Within the brief span of three finely wro... has given us a compelling apologetic for ... wells of Deuteronomy. This little book is so seminal, so convincing, so winsome, so bracing and salutary-- that is should be commended as an indispensable read to all who aspire to preach the Word.

R. Kent Hughes,
Senior Pastor Emeritus, College Church, Wheaton

This is a potent and perceptive little book which enables the hard-working, humble preacher of scripture to take heart and stand tall in his calling. It contains a tonic which some of us need to take every Sunday morning!

John Benton,
Editor, *Evangelicals Now*

My heart was warmed, my mind informed and my will challenged ... read it, practice it and give a copy to your best friends to do the same.

Ján Henžel,
President, Evangelical Free Church in Slovakia,
Senior lecturer, Matej Bel University.

This is a great read. Plenty of books give tips and anecdotes for preachers. But this one gives us pastors a massive encouragement to make preaching a priority and to keep it there. There's also encouragement to keep Scripture at the centre of preaching and to preach book by book. What I especially like is that Christopher Ash uses the Scriptures itself to make his point. That is, he models the preacher's principle of acting with confidence in God's word. I read this book on a weekend when I preached three sermons in two hemispheres – the book was an encouragement to bound from plane to pulpit.

David Burke,
Orchard Road Presbyterian Church, Singapore

THE PRIORITY OF
PREACHING

Christopher Ash

PTMEDIA

CHRISTIAN
FOCUS

Copyright © Christopher Ash

ISBN 978-1-84550-464-9

10 9 8 7 6 5 4 3 2 1

Published in 2009
reprinted in 2010
by
Christian Focus Publications,
Geanies House, Fearn, Ross-shire,
IV20 1TW, Scotland, Great Britain
with
Proclamation Trust Media,
Willcox House, 140-148 Borough High Street,
London, SE1 1LB, England, Great Britain.
www.proctrust.org.uk

www.christianfocus.com

Cover design by Moose77.com
Printed by Norhaven, Denmark

Contents

Dedication...7

Series Preface..9

Introduction: For Discouraged Preachers................................11

1.   The Authority of the Preached Word.......................................15

2.   Preaching that Transforms the Church.............................. 45

3.   Preaching that Mends a Broken World.............................75

Appendix: Give God the Microphone!
(Seven blessings of consecutive expository preaching) 107

Dedication

To Mark Ashton,
under whose care I came to faith in Christ,
and under whose leadership I learned
the priority of preaching from a pastor's heart
amidst the pressures of local church life.

Series Preface

This is the second in a series of books which looks at the culture and context of preaching and teaching God's Word. We need help not just in 'how to preach Bible books', but clarity on the point and purpose of preaching and teaching. The books in this series will be short and accessible, ideal for personal use, group study or for training. The following titles are planned:

Bible Delight: Heartbeat of the Word of God (published in 2008)
The Potential of a Praying Church
The Pastoral Preacher
Training Preachers: what it takes to make a preacher
The Lifelong Preacher: keeping fresh, keeping focused

Christopher Ash's book, *Bible Delight: Heartbeat of the Word of God* is an excellent foundation for the series, getting to the heart of our motivation to preach and teach. We are encouraged by the strong response to this book.

In his second book in the series, *The Priority of Preaching*, Christopher offers a thoroughly biblical argument for the priority of preaching as the vital life of the church. His material

9

is rooted in the 'normal' church – local church pastors and teachers – grafting at the chalk face of Christian mission.

This material was first presented at the 2008 Evangelical Ministry Assembly in London. For those of us who were there, there was tangible excitement as we came to see how preaching in the local church is central to God's plan for mending a broken world. Many discouraged preachers were encouraged, and returned to their churches with renewed zeal to preach God's Word. It is our prayer that God will use this short book, not only to encourage and inspire those of us who are preachers, but to raise up a whole new generation of preachers whom God will use to mend this broken world.

David Jackman and Robin Sydserff
Series Editors, London & Edinburgh, March 2009

Introduction:

For Discouraged Preachers

This book is written for preachers and aspiring preachers. It is also written for listeners. In his magnificent account of Calvin's preaching, T.H.L. Parker writes, 'The preacher is only the half of the Church's activity of proclamation …. The assumption seems to be that, whereas the preacher is really doing something, the people have a passive role, like so many jugs waiting to be filled. … Anyone who has regularly preached over many years but then has been a member of a congregation for some time, would (if he had strong views on preaching) be hard put to it to decide which was the more demanding, preaching well or listening properly.'[1] I hope that as sermon listeners listen in to this conversation between one preacher and his fellow-preachers, they may be helped in the task of learning to listen well to sermons, and of knowing how best to encourage their preachers.

Some years ago I remember attending a large conference of ministers. At the time I was pastoring an ordinary local church, which consisted of mainly ordinary people in a very ordinary place, a village in Eastern England. Sad to say, all I can remember of the conference is impressive speakers who all seemed (to my

1. T.H.L. Parker, *Calvin's Preaching* (T & T Clark, 1992) p. 48

jaded eyes) to be tall, handsome, successful – everything I was not. Above all, they seemed to talk a lot about doing 'strategic' work for the gospel of Christ. It all seemed very strategic. They were clearly strategic people in strategic places doing strategic ministry. I, however, being of a melancholic disposition, was quite sure I was not a strategic person, nor was I in a strategic place, and I was most certainly not doing strategic ministry. As I left the conference, like a dog with its tail between its legs, I wondered if it was really worth preparing for Sunday's preaching.

At the Cornhill Training Course we get a few random applications from people who know nothing about us, but have somehow stumbled upon us on the internet. One of my favourites was from a man who said he had heard of Cornhill, 'At Pastor Benny Hinn's crusade in Nigeria'. Those familiar with Benny Hinn and with the Cornhill Training Course will know that this is unlikely to be true. In answer to the question of what he most wanted to do with the rest of his life, this applicant wrote, in capital letters, 'TO BE A WORLD-RENOWNED PREACHER AND TEACHER OF THE WORD OF GOD.' Yes, I thought, we have all dreamed of that, just as we may have wanted to ask the LORD Jesus to sit at his right hand or his left in the Kingdom. But that kind of request has already been tried and it wasn't well received by Jesus (Matt. 20:20-28).

This little book is written for ordinary ministers who preach regularly to ordinary people in ordinary places, who may dream of being world-renowned but are going to be spared that fate. Most of us preach in gatherings that are smaller than we would wish and tougher than we might have hoped when we entered pastoral ministry. Sometimes we are jaded by opposition, or by defections, or just by the sheer unrelenting slog of church leadership. There is a voice on our shoulders who whispers as we prepare, and then as we preach, 'Is it really worth it? Why not busk it this week? Who would notice? After all, you're fooling yourself if you think you're doing anything significant.' The devil will throw at us every distraction and discouragement in his arsenal.

Introduction

The three chapters of this book were originally given as addresses at the 25th Evangelical Ministry Assembly in June 2008. I hope their effect on delegates was different from the effect on me of the conference I remembered from an earlier year. The addresses were given, and the book is written, from the conviction that the sermons you and I preach week by week in ordinary local churches are more significant than most conference addresses even if they were to be recorded and played back all over the world. My task is to persuade (or at least unsettle) those doubtful about preaching, and to deepen the conviction of those already converted to the priority of preaching. Above all, I want to encourage us to our desks, our prayer, our preparation, and our love for people, with a new spring in our steps as we labour at loving people by preaching to them week by week. My prayer is that this book will encourage the discouraged preacher to persevere with fresh zeal and enthusiasm, because I have convinced you that this Sunday men and women can hear the voice of the living God from your mouth.

The main influences that have fed into this book have been of two kinds. In terms of books, my studies of Deuteronomy owe much to Gordon McConville's outstandingly clear and perceptively theological commentary[2] and I have also gained much by reading or re-reading the various books on preaching noted in footnotes, especially John Stott's *I believe in Preaching*.[3] Pastorally, I owe a great debt to the fellowship of faithful pastor-teachers and preachers whom The Proclamation Trust seeks to serve, and in particular to Dick Lucas, whose expository ministry was the inspiration for The Proclamation Trust and to David Jackman, my predecessor and the founder-director of the Cornhill Training Course, to whose work in equipping expository preachers we all owe so much.

---

2. J.G. McConville, *Deuteronomy* (IVP Apollos, 2002)
3. John Stott, *I believe in Preaching* (Hodder and Stoughton, 1982)

1

The Authority of
the Preached Word

Deuteronomy 18:9-22

[9]When you enter the land the LORD your God is giving you, do not learn to imitate the detestable ways of the nations there. [10]Let no one be found among you who sacrifices his son or daughter in the fire, who practices divination or sorcery, interprets omens, engages in witchcraft, [11]or casts spells, or who is a medium or spiritist or who consults the dead. [12]Anyone who does these things is detestable to the LORD, and because of these detestable practices the LORD your God will drive out those nations before you. [13]You must be blameless before the LORD your God.

[14]The nations you will dispossess listen to those who practice sorcery or divination. But as for you, the LORD your God has not permitted you to do so. [15]The LORD your God will raise up for you a prophet like me from among your own brothers. You must listen to him. [16]For this is what you asked of the LORD your God at Horeb on the day of the assembly when you said, "Let us not hear the voice of the LORD our God nor see this great fire anymore, or we will die."

[17]The LORD said to me: "What they say is good. [18]I will raise up for them a prophet like you from among their brothers; I will

put my words in his mouth, and he will tell them everything I command him. [19]If anyone does not listen to my words that the prophet speaks in my name, I myself will call him to account. [20]But a prophet who presumes to speak in my name anything I have not commanded him to say, or a prophet who speaks in the name of other gods, must be put to death."

[21]You may say to yourselves, "How can we know when a message has not been spoken by the LORD ?" [22]If what a prophet proclaims in the name of the LORD does not take place or come true, that is a message the LORD has not spoken. That prophet has spoken presumptuously. Do not be afraid of him.

This chapter is an exposition (with detours) of three words spoken in the Old Testament and repeated in the New: 'listen to him'. In the NIV these are the last three words of Deuteronomy 18:15: 'The LORD your God will raise up for you a prophet like me from among your own brothers. You must *listen to him.*' In the New Testament they are spoken by God about Jesus on the Mount of Transfiguration: 'This is my Son, whom I love. *Listen to him!*' (Mark 9:7). We will come to the New Testament later, but I want to start with Deuteronomy.

My thesis in this first chapter is that we must listen today to the voice of the Christian preacher because he is the prophet in our generation as Moses was in his. God says of this prophet, 'I will put my words in his mouth' (Deut. 18:18). Again, it is my thesis that the Christian preacher today can speak the words God puts in his mouth, the very words of God. And therefore it is imperative we listen to him. To state my thesis boldly like this invites incredulity in my readers. What does he think he is doing making such absurd claims? What kind of doctrine of inspiration does he hold, or of contemporary prophecy? Although you may be thinking like this, bear with me as I develop the thesis.

THE ISSUE: WHY PREACH?

The Evangelical Ministry Assembly was one of the influences that contributed to the birth of The Proclamation Trust in 1986, dedicated to the encouragement of expository preaching ministry in the UK and beyond. Those who chose the name called it The *Proclamation* Trust. They didn't call it 'The Discussion Trust', 'The Apologetics Trust', 'The Intelligent Defence of Christianity (to its cultured despisers) Trust'[1]. They didn't even call it 'The Bible Study Trust', 'The Bible Reading Trust' or 'The Bible Teaching Trust'. They called it 'The *Proclamation* Trust'. I take it they did so because they wanted to headline the unique significance of the public expository preaching of the word of Christ. They wanted to be a fellowship to encourage expository preachers in a demanding work. They wanted to signal their conviction that public preaching deserves the highest priority among all the different expressions of word ministry in the church. I believe they were right then, and that it is still a good name now.

Preaching has never lacked for mocking opponents. Anthony Trollope in 1857 wrote, 'There is, perhaps, no greater hardship at present inflicted on mankind in civilized and free countries, than the necessity of listening to sermons'; he goes on to describe the 'preaching clergyman' as 'the bore of the age' and laments his '… imperfect sentences … repeated phrases …false pathos … drawlings and denouncings …'[2]. In his novel *A Passage to India*, written in the 1920s, E.M. Forster too reveals his scepticism about Christian preaching. His character Mrs Moore is reflecting on her fright at the echo she heard in the Marabar cave ('Boum'). As she reflects, 'suddenly, at the edge of her mind, Religion appeared, poor little talkative Christianity, and she knew that all its divine words from "Let there be light" to "It is finished" only amounted to "Boum".' This is where we get Forster's famous jibe ('poor little talkative Christianity').[3] Is that all we preachers are, Sunday by Sunday, just poor little talkative chatter-boxes carrying on a long tradition of 'poor little talkative Christianity', amounting to nothing more than a meaningless echo in a cave?

1.   cf. Schleiermacher's famous *Speeches on Religion to its Cultured Despisers* (1799)
2.   Anthony Trollope, *Barchester Towers* (my edition, Oxford University Press, 1991), p. 52f
3.   E.M. Forster, *A Passage to India* (First published 1924. My edition, Penguin Books, 1985), p. 146

The Priority of Preaching

A few years ago I read the obituary of Albert Marshall, who died aged 108. Marshall was the last surviving British Cavalryman to ride his horse into action on the Western Front in the First World War. Those were the days when General Haig and others really believed that cavalry would win the war. A mounted charge with swords or lances, moving quickly and breaking through the infantry lines, would carry all before them, just as they had done in century after century since the Greek squadrons of Xenophon. But in an age of high-explosive shells and chlorine gas, cavalry were hopeless, outdated, a relic of a bygone age of warfare. Many think preaching is like that, a heroic attempt by nostalgic Christians to sustain the methods of a bygone age.

It is never easy to write in defence of preaching. Whenever preachers write about preaching, they are invariably full of gloom and always lament the current state of affairs. Back in 1907 P.T. Forsyth laments 'the absence of the note of authority' in the preaching of his day.[4] In 1954 W.E. Sangster begins his book *The Craft of the Sermon*: 'Preaching is in the shadows. The world does not believe in it. Perhaps it never did believe in it much, but in England, at least, it believed in it once more than it believes in it now'.[5] In 1958 Donald Coggan (later Archbishop of Canterbury) comments that the devil has effectively silenced many preachers, and has demoralised those who continue to preach. They go to their pulpits, he writes, 'as men who have lost their battle before they start; the ground of conviction has slipped from under their feet'.[6] In 1962 John Stott wrote 'The prophets of doom in today's Church are confidently predicting that the day of preaching is over. It is a dying art, they say, an outmoded form of communication, "an echo from an abandoned past".'[7] He notes that 'to preach' is defined in

---

4.   P.T. Forsyth, *Positive Preaching and the Modern Mind* (3rd Edition. London: Independent Press, 1949), p. 27

5.   W.E. Sangster, *The Craft of the Sermon* (London: Epworth Press, 1954), p. 1

6.   Donald F. Coggan, *Stewards of Grace* (Hodder and Stoughton, 1958) p. 13, quoted in John R.W. Stott, *I believe in Preaching* (Hodder and Stoughton, 1962), p. 50

7.   John R.W. Stott, *I believe in Preaching* (Hodder and Stoughton, 1962), p. 50

The Authority of the Preached Word

Chambers Dictionary as 'to give advice in an offensive, tedious or obtrusive manner', and to be 'sermonic' means to inflict on someone a patronising harangue.[8] In 1980 Haddon Robinson laments that his book *Expository Preaching* 'may have been written for a depressed market. Not everyone agrees that expository preaching – or any sort of preaching, for that matter – is an urgent need of the church. The word is out in some circles that preaching should be abandoned. The moving finger has passed it by and now points to other methods and ministries that are more "effective" and in tune with the times'.[9] Alec Motyer, in his Foreword to Haddon Robinson, comments (not very encouragingly, for a Foreword!) that the appearance of a book on Expository Preaching 'is … likely to provoke a yawn. For there are those who have come to regard preaching as outmoded and irrelevant, superseded by other means of communicating the gospel such as dialogue, discussion and drama'.[10] And in 1996, Peter Adam writes that 'the general mood of our church life and world is against preaching'.[11]

If there is one thing all books about preaching have in common, it would seem to be this all-pervasive gloom. I've not yet read one author who begins by saying, 'Isn't it wonderful there are so many fine preachers out there and so many eager and attentive congregations?' If there were, I suppose we would all be so cheerfully complacent we would not bother to buy their book. So I suppose I had better join the gloom, in the hopes that you will think it worth buying this book. But at least we gloom-merchants can claim to have the apostle Paul on our side. Right back in 2 Timothy Paul tells us that these last days (between Jesus' first coming and his return) will be difficult; people will not endure sound teaching, but with itching ears will pile up teachers to tell them what they want to

---

8.   John R.W. Stott, *I believe in Preaching* (Hodder and Stoughton, 1962), p. 52

9.   Haddon W. Robinson, *Expository Preaching: Principles and Practice* (IVP, 1980), p. 15

10.   J.A. Motyer, Foreword to Haddon W. Robinson *Expository Preaching: Principles and Practice* (IVP, 1980), p. i

11.   Peter Adam, *Speaking God's Words: A practical theology of preaching* (IVP, 1996), p. 9

hear (2 Tim. 3:1-9; 4:3, 4). Until Jesus returns there will be lots of bad preachers and lots of bad congregations.

IS PREACHING MORE IMPORTANT THAN OTHER 'WORD MINISTRIES'? So scepticism about preaching is not new. But I want us to consider one particular slant on this scepticism, which is a scepticism from within the evangelical constituency, among those of us who are convinced that prayer and the ministry of the word are the prime and apostolic priority for the pastor-teacher. Are we right to say that preaching should have a position of primacy amongst all the ministries of the word? I remember the old illustration used to encourage one to one Bible reading, in which two strategies are tried for pouring water into a tray of glasses. First we try pouring from a jug high above the tray; the water splashes around, and not much of it goes into the glasses. Then we carefully pour into each glass individually, with much more success. We were encouraged to deduce that one to one Bible reading was probably better than preaching. If we really believe this is true, we will probably not work very hard at preparing for Sunday. But although one to one Bible reading is of great value (and I thank God for those who have given this kind of pastoral care to me), I want to question whether this is true. Quite apart from the dubious procedure of deducing doctrine from an illustration, I want to suggest biblical and theological reasons for affirming the priority of preaching.

Scepticism about the priority of preaching has been expressed as follows: 'I've never really been comfortable with the evangelical emphasis on preaching sermons, and never quite understood why we make so much more of this form rather than of other forms of teaching.'[12] By 'preaching' the writer explains that he means what he calls "pulpiteering', as opposed to private and personal ministry through, for example, conversation or Bible study groups'. The word 'pulpiteering' sounds vaguely disreputable, something you

---

12.   Gordon Cheng, *The Briefing* Issue 353 (February 2008) p. 5

wouldn't want to do with granny in the room, a verbal cousin of 'domineering' or 'profiteering'; and like 'fundamentalism', almost a form of ecclesiastical terrorism. We imagine the conversation: 'What are you doing this Sunday?' (Confidential whisper in reply): 'Don't tell granny, but I'm pulpiteering!'

But it's a serious question. Are we right to understand preaching as 'the central part of our ministry of the word'[13] (Peter Adam) and 'the most excellent' part of the pastor's work[14] (Richard Baxter)? Or ought we to see it as just one among equals along with other Bible-teaching ministries? That would certainly feel more democratic, in tune with the spirit of the age. Is it true, as Charles Simeon put it, that 'God himself speaks to us by the preacher,' and that 'If (preachers) preach what is founded on the Scriptures, their word, as far as it is agreeable to the mind of God, is to be considered as God's?'[15]

BUILDING THE CASE FROM THE BOOK OF DEUTERONOMY
The Question of Deuteronomy: the Church after Moses
I want to approach this question of the priority of preaching from Deuteronomy. I have chosen Deuteronomy because it seems to me that Deuteronomy gives us God's mandate for preaching. It's a curious book, in some ways, because nothing really happens in it.

There's some history recounted that's already happened, and already been recorded in Exodus, Leviticus and Numbers (Deut. 1:6-3:29). There are some laws repeated that have already been given (more or less) in Exodus, Leviticus and Deuteronomy[16]. The only thing that happens is that Moses dies. It wouldn't make a great action movie!

---

13. Peter Adam, *Speaking God's Words: a practical theology of preaching* (IVP, 1996) p.72
14. Richard Baxter, *The Reformed Pastor* (London: James Nisbet and Co, 1860) p. 128
15. Charles Simeon, 'Directions how to hear sermons' in *Let Wisdom Judge* (London: Inter-Varsity Fellowship, 1959), p. 189
16. Of course there are some laws unique to Deuteronomy, and some that are significant variants of the other laws. But it hardly seems enough to justify a completely new book of the Bible.

The death of Moses overshadows the book. Even in chapter 1 Moses reminds them that the LORD had said to him, 'You shall not enter (the land)' (Deut. 1:37). Joshua is mentioned first in Deuteronomy 1:38, and every time he is mentioned thereafter (e.g. Deut. 3:21) it's a reminder that Moses is going to die. Moses keeps repeating to them that he does not have permission to enter the land with them. We find it movingly in Deuteronomy 3:23-28, 'At that time I pleaded with the LORD: "O Sovereign LORD, … Let me go over and see the good land …" But because of you the LORD was angry with me and would not listen to me. …' Moses then says it again in Deuteronomy 4:21, 'The LORD was angry with me because of you, and he solemnly swore that I would not cross the Jordan and enter the good land …'

This theme music of Moses' imminent death becomes insistent in the last four chapters. In Deuteronomy 31:2 Moses says to the people, 'I am now a hundred and twenty years old and I am no longer able to lead you. The LORD has said to me, "You shall not cross the Jordan."' Then in Deuteronomy 31:14 we read, 'The LORD said to Moses, "Now the day of your death is near. Call Joshua and present yourselves at the Tent of Meeting, where I will commission him."' Two verses later we read, 'And the LORD said to Moses, "You are going to rest with your fathers…"'

After Moses' song in chapter 32, we read, 'On that same day the LORD told Moses, "Go up into the Abarim Range to Mount Nebo in Moab, across from Jericho, and view Canaan, the land I am giving the Israelites as their own possession. There on the mountain that you have climbed you will die and be gathered to your people… you will see the land only from a distance; you will not enter the land I am giving to the people of Israel' (Deut. 32:48-52). Chapter 33 begins, 'This is the blessing that Moses the man of God pronounced on the Israelites before his death' (Deut. 33:1). And then in chapter 34 he dies.

I suggest that the big issue in Deuteronomy is this: how are the covenant people going to continue after the covenant mediator is gone? How are the people of God to continue to be the people of God in the absence of their founding leader? How is the covenant God to govern his people after the covenant mediator is dead, the one through whose ministry they have been redeemed?

The Answer of Deuteronomy: The people of God under the preached word of God
And I suggest that the answer of Deuteronomy, in a nutshell, is this: the covenant will continue as the covenant God assembles his covenant people under his preached covenant word. Deuteronomy is the mandate for the people of God to assemble under the preached word of God, or to be more accurate, the written word preached. This is why Deuteronomy is not really a law book, but a preaching book.

Politically, the people continue under Joshua's lead. Spiritually, they continue because the LORD is with them. But instrumentally, they continue because a series of prophets preaches to them; these are the instruments God uses.

Deuteronomy is a wonderful book to preach. For when we preach Deuteronomy we preach the preaching that Moses preached, although we may need to make it clear to our hearers that this is what we are doing. I once thought I would cleverly introduce a sermon from Deuteronomy by saying, 'I hope you won't mind if this week I preach you a sermon someone else has preached before.' I thought this was rather clever, until a man came up to me at the end and innocently asked, 'Who did preach that sermon first?' So clearly my little bit of fun was neither as funny nor as clear as I had hoped. I was trying to be much too clever for my own good!

The first truth I want to develop from Deuteronomy is this:

A. THE PREACHER EXERCISES THE AUTHORITY OF CHRIST IN THE CHURCH
This sounds dangerous. It will sound even more dangerous if I say, 'The *prophetic* preacher exercises the authority of Christ in the church.' So let me develop it carefully in two stages.

The Priority of Preaching

1. *Under the old covenant, God governed his people by the written word preached by the prophets*

   (a) *The primacy of the prophet in the people of God.*

Deuteronomy is the book of the prototypical prophet. It begins, 'These are the words Moses spoke ...' (Deut. 1:1). It ends, 'Since then, no prophet has risen in Israel like Moses ...' (Deut. 34:10). In between the beginning and the end, Moses prophesies; that is, he speaks God's words, as the covenant mediator and preacher. Although Deuteronomy is classified with the Torah, it is really the Covenant preached by the prototypical prophet. Although Moses was a great leader, the Old Testament doesn't call him a king. Although he came from a priestly family, he is not remembered as a priest. He is remembered as the first and great prophet of Israel: 'The LORD used a *prophet* to bring Israel up from Egypt' (Hosea 12:13). What later became 'the law and the prophets' began in Deuteronomy with 'the law preached by the prototypical prophet'. This signals to us the primacy of the prophet in the people of God. In Deuteronomy 1:9-18, Moses delegates government to wise, just judges. But the hard cases still come to him (Deut. 1:17). So what will happen when he is gone? Who will be God's vicar in Israel? To whom should we listen? Answer: the prophet like Moses.

This answer is given negatively in Deut.13, where three different siren voices are heard. All three have the same message: 'Let us follow/go and worship other gods' (Deut. 13:2, 6, 13). But they are of different levels of danger. At the end is the least dangerous (vv. 12-18): 'wicked men' (ESV 'certain worthless fellows') – random bad people. Don't listen to them. Before them (vv. 6-11) are more dangerous people, more dangerous because they are closer to us: your brother, your son, your daughter, the wife you embrace, the very close friend – don't let them lure you away. Don't listen to them. But the primary danger, with which the chapter begins (vv. 1-5), is 'a prophet or one who foretells by dreams' (ESV 'a dreamer of dreams') (v. 1). They are the most dangerous because they claim their words are God's words. The false prophet is the greatest danger because the true prophet is the highest authority. A forged £50 note is more dangerous than a false penny.

The answer is given positively in the section from Deuteronomy 16:18–18:22, a section that deals with the government of Israel. The section begins (Deut. 16:18–17:7) at the lowest level, with the local officials. Next up (Deut. 17:8-13) are the central officials. Next up (Deut. 17:14-20) is the king, who is important but not nearly as important as most kings think. Next up (Deut. 18:1-8) are the priests. And finally, at the head of the government of the people of God, we have the voice of God through the prophet (Deut. 18:9-22). To whom should we listen? Answer: Don't listen to divination, fortune telling, omens, sorcery, mediums (Deut. 18:9-14). But do listen to the prophet like Moses. This means a succession of prophets, generation after generation, so that there is 'a prophet like Moses' in each generation. The saying, 'Who, being called to be a preacher, would stoop to be a king?' is attributed to Thomas Carlyle. We could certainly say in ancient Israel: Who, being called to be a prophet, would stoop to be a king?

And so it continued through Israel's history. At their best the judges functioned rather like prophets, so that the people are condemned because, 'They would not *listen* to their judges' (Judg. 2:17). The priest Eli is rebuked by 'a man of God' (1 Sam. 2:27), which means a prophet.[17] King Saul has to listen to Samuel the prophet ('Listen now to the message from the LORD', 1 Sam. 15:1). After his adultery with Bathsheba, the only person with the authority to rebuke King David is Nathan the prophet (2 Sam. 12:1ff). To whom does King Hezekiah turn in his time of need? To Isaiah the prophet (2 Kings 19:2). It is prophets like Elijah and Elisha who anoint and dethrone kings (e.g. 1 Kings 19:15f). The people who matter most in Israel are neither priests nor kings, but prophets.

17. John Woodhouse, *1 Samuel: Looking for a Leader* (Crossway Books, 2008), p. 562n1

*(b) The Authority of God is exercised not by the written word
but by the written word preached*

This is very significant. It means that the authority of God was
mediated in Israel not by the written word, but by the written
word *preached*. The word of the covenant was written on tablets
of stone. But those written words must be preached. We see
both written word and preached word in Deuteronomy. The
'Ten Words' of the covenant were 'inscribed by the finger of
God' (Deut. 9:10), but they were preached by Moses. Moses'
preaching was written on large stones (Deut. 27:1-8); the law
was written by Moses (Deut. 31:9). But it was to be read and
preached in every generation by the prophets.

And so began that great prophetic succession by whose
mouths the LORD preached the covenant to his people. As
O. Palmer Robertson puts it, 'This small single voice replaces
all the fearsome signs that accompanied the theophany of
Sinai. The smoking, shaking mountain ... now finds its
equivalent in the gentle voice of the brother speaking among
brothers'.[18] These were 'the eyes of the people', as Isaiah puts it
(Isa. 29:10-14), and they were the watchmen (Jer. 6:17).

This is why the test of obedience to God was whether
or not they listened to the prophet. To be stiff-necked is not
to give ear to the prophets (Neh. 9:29). When Jesus sums up
rebellion against God he calls it 'persecuting the prophets'
(Matt. 5:12), being 'the sons of those who murdered the
prophets' (Matt. 23:31) or being 'the city that kills the prophets'
(Luke 13:34).

The written covenant was the anchor that tied the true
prophet into the succession of true prophets. True prophets
were preachers of the written covenant. Both were needed.
Sometimes the word was written but not preached. But without
the preacher the word gathers dust in a forgotten corner of
the temple, to be discovered by the builders (as in Josiah's

---

18.   O. Palmer Robertson, *The Christ of the Prophets* (Presbyterian and Reformed, 2004), p. 26

reign, 2 Kings 22). At other times some kind of 'word' may be preached, but this preached 'word' is divorced from the written word. And yet without the written word, the prophet becomes simply a 'dreamer of dreams' (e.g. Deut. 13:1ff). Neither the written word alone, nor the prophet alone, is sufficient, but rather the written word preached.

God did not just give them the book. He gave them preachers of the book so that face to face they could be taught, challenged, rebuked and exhorted to repentance and faith. And therefore one of the worst things God could do was to stop speaking to his people by the prophets, as he had almost done before the time of Samuel, when things were very dark and everyone did what was right in his own eyes (e.g. Judg. 17:6; 21:25) and the word of the LORD was rare (1 Sam. 3:1). The word was there, written on the tablets in the Ark; but nobody preached it. In the time of Amos God threatens 'a famine of hearing the words of the LORD' (Amos 8:11f.); this famine is not so much the absence of prophets to tell them the future; it is more the absence of prophets to preach to them the covenant. Later, at the time of Psalm 74:9 ('there is no longer any prophet'), they didn't say, 'Oh, well, it doesn't matter because we've got the book.' They said, 'There is no longer any prophet … How long, O LORD …?' because the loving authority of God is exercised by the written word preached. The preaching of the prophets was gradually collected so that the written word grew. But at every stage God governed his people by those who preached the written word, not just by the written testimony in the ark or on scrolls.

Preaching is culturally-neutral

It is worth pausing to consider why God exercised his authority in Israel not by the written word, but by the written word preached. Every culture knows what it is to sit and listen to an authoritative human being speak. That is not culturally specific. You don't need to be literate to do that. You don't need to be educated to do that. You don't need to be fluent or confident in debate to do that. Every human being can do that. And that's what preaching is. Of course we clothe preaching in cultural garments. We may slip into preaching in a churchy way, or a preachy way, or in the language of the ghetto, or in a stilted way, or in a way that sounds like a commentary extract being read. We ought not to do this. But preaching in its essence is an authorized human being speaking the words of God to listening human beings; and every culture understands that.

An interactive Bible study is not culturally-neutral. To sit around drinking coffee with a book open, reading and talking about that book in a way that forces me to keep looking at the book and finding my place and showing a high level of mental agility, functional literacy, spoken coherence and fluency, that is something only some of the human race are comfortable doing. Not everyone feels comfortable when the bright spark in the corner pipes up, 'Ah, yes, but I was wondering about the significance of the word 'However' in verse 3b. What do you think about that?' Some of us love that kind of seminar interaction, but many do not. For those who can do it, it may well be profitable; but many people can't, and just feel daunted or excluded by the exercise.

In some churches we have slipped into assuming that personal Bible reading and one-to-one Bible studies and Bible study groups are the normative way for Christian people to hear the word of God. This, we say, is what a healthy Christian life looks like. But in defining the Christian life like this we may unwittingly have alienated the illiterate, the functionally illiterate, the less-educated, those less confident in studying a text. I wonder if, quite unintentionally, we may have contributed to making some of our churches more monocultural than they might otherwise be. Paradoxically it is not that preaching is culturally outmoded, but rather that the study of written Bible texts is culturally narrow.

So how are we to reach those for whom this kind of study is culturally alien? We have two options: theatre and preaching. By 'theatre' I mean entertainment, whether it be by the liturgical colour and drama of high church ritual, or by entrancing music or by entertaining anecdotes. Just as the Roman emperors reckoned the people would be happy so long as they had 'bread and circuses' so church leaders may rely on the entertainment culture of the circus. Peter Adam makes the point that from the seventh century to the twelfth century there was a movement that said that ordinary people could not understand preaching, so the best way to communicate with them was by statues, stained-glass windows and pictures. But, as the Reformers discovered, it failed. '(I)t produced people who knew the gospel stories, but did not know the gospel; people who knew what had happened, but who did not know the meaning of it'.[19]

The alternative to theatre is preaching, the simple activity of a man speaking the words of God face to face with men and women. This is how God used John Wesley, George Whitefield, Charles Spurgeon, F. B. Meyer, Billy Graham to reach the masses. We have no need to be defensive about preaching: it speaks to every culture.

What is the place of Bible study groups?
I suggest that we ought to rethink the place and purpose of Bible study groups, for two reasons. The first is that, all too often, a Bible study group is a place where discussion substitutes for submission to the word of God. One pastor wrote to me to say, 'I have long felt that … for all the ways in which home groups look as though God's people are coming under the Word of God, my experience is that the home group is the classic arena in which God's people in fact sit above the Word of God.' He went on to say that they were experimenting in their church with a shift of focus. In their small groups they take the passage that had been preached the previous Sunday, make sure they understand it, and then devote most of their energies 'into holding one another accountable for how we live this passage out in the week ahead (that is, we try and use small groups to underline rather than undermine our sense of being God's people, coming under his word and holding one another

---

19.   Peter Adam, *Speaking God's Words: a practical theology of preaching* (IVP, 1996) p. 168

accountable to what He is saying to us).' In this model the role of the small group is the application of the Bible passage rather than the interpretation and understanding of the passage. Of course it is rarely quite as simple as this; there is a valuable place for clarification of meaning in a well-led small group, and this clarification overlaps with working out responsible application to us. But it is a shift of focus that I commend.

The second reason to rethink Bible study groups is a concern to model the Christian life in a way which does not exclude the less confident, less fluent, those less at home studying a written text. This concern is not confined to those who are actually illiterate. One minister in a university town was telling me that his church attracts students from two universities, one more academic and distinguished than the other. When their main midweek meeting was a teaching meeting led by a member of staff, students from both campuses attended. But when they switched and made it a Bible study group meeting, quite suddenly almost all the students from the less academic university ceased to attend. Although these were university students, they were not comfortable sitting in a group studying a written text. We could remodel our groups so that in general we teach the Bible text from the front and then use the small group time, firstly to make sure everyone has understood the passage, but mainly to interact with one another as to what we are going to do about it by way of trusting obedience.

2. *Under the new covenant, Christ governs his people by the written word preached by preachers*

It is time now to draw some careful lines from the prophets to Christian preachers.

(a) *The progressive revelatory role of the prophets is fulfilled in Christ the Prophet*

The prophets held together two roles, and so far I have only focused on one. They were preachers of the covenant word. But they were also progressive revealers of the promised Christ.

The Authority of the Preached Word

As Calvin puts it, they 'express more clearly what Moses says more obscurely about Christ and his grace,'[20] as the Spirit of Christ within them predicted the sufferings of Christ and the subsequent glory (1 Pet. 1:10f).

The book of Deuteronomy sets up brilliantly the tension between these two roles. On the one hand Moses says that God 'will raise up for you a prophet like me' (Deut. 18:15), where, as we have seen, the natural meaning is a succession of prophets like Moses so that in each generation they know to whom they must listen. But, on the other hand, the book closes by saying, 'Since then, no prophet has risen in Israel like Moses ...' (Deut. 34:10). So are there or are there not prophets like Moses in the succeeding generations of Israel's history? 'A prophet like Moses' or 'No prophet like Moses': which is it to be?

In one sense there were plenty of prophets like Moses, who preached the covenant faithfully. This great succession of prophets proclaimed that there is one true God, the LORD, the covenant God, the God of Abraham, Isaac and Jacob, the God of the Exodus. They declared that their hearers must repent, they must trust this God and bow before him with the obedience of faith (cf. Rom. 1:5; 16:26). Samuel, Elijah, Isaiah, and many others did this. They were 'like Moses' in that they faithfully preached the covenant that Moses preached in Deuteronomy.

So how were they not like Moses? The clue is in Deuteronomy 34:10-12, '... no prophet has risen in Israel like Moses, whom the LORD knew face to face, who did all those miraculous signs and wonders the LORD sent him to do in Egypt – to Pharaoh and to all his officials and to his whole land. For no-one has ever shown the mighty power or performed the awesome deeds that Moses did in the sight of all Israel.' There were prophets who spoke and preached like Moses; but there was no prophet who redeemed like Moses, into whom they were 'baptised'[21] in

---

20. quoted from *Twelve Minor Prophets* in O.Palmer Robertson, *The Christ of the Prophets* (Presbyterian and Reformed, 2004), p. 123

21. 1 Corinthians 10:2

the great redeeming events of the Exodus. For that Redeemer Prophet (the Prophet with a capital 'P') they waited, whose mighty redemption would make the Exodus seem small by comparison.

Both Peter and Stephen quote this passage in Deuteronomy 18 (in Acts 3:22f. and Acts 7:37, 52). And both of them understand it to refer both to the succession of prophets, and to the expectation of a final Prophet.

The people asked John the Baptist, 'Are you *the* Prophet?' (John 1:21, 25) But he wasn't. He was indeed a prophet, and more than a prophet, says Jesus (Matt. 11:9ff.), but he is not *the* Prophet. But of Jesus they said, 'This is indeed the Prophet who is to come into the world!' (John 6:14), and 'This really is the prophet.' (John 7:40). On the mount of Transfiguration Peter, James and John heard the voice from the Majestic Glory (2 Pet. 1:17). And when they heard that voice, it echoed the words from Deuteronomy 18:15, 'Stop talking, stop discussing: *listen to him*!' For centuries he had sent his servants the prophets, and now he has sent his Son (Matt. 21:33-44). 'In the past God spoke to our forefathers through the prophets at many times and in various ways, but in these last days he has spoken to us by his Son ...' who is the mediator of a new and better covenant, in whom we have a redemption deeper than the redemption from Egypt, the forgiveness of our sins (Heb. 1:1-2).

And so the prophetic succession comes to its climax in Jesus Christ. How does God govern his church? He governs it by the Prophet like Moses, the Mediator between God and people (1 Tim. 2:5): we must listen to him.

(b)   But Christ the Prophet is no longer here!

But the problem is, Christ the Prophet is not here in our churches. It would be fine to say God governs his church by the voice of Christ, if Christ were here. But he's not. That's the biggest problem faced by every church leader, the physical absence of Jesus Christ. Of course we believe he is with us by his Spirit. But that doesn't help much when it comes to governing the local church – as many pastors know to their cost. Faced with different members of an eldership, a church council, a church leadership, all claiming that the risen Jesus is on their side, who is to adjudicate, since he is not physically here? We face the same problem faced by Israel after Moses: there will be lots of voices claiming to speak for God, but which of them really does? The problem of false prophecy in the Old Testament continued in the New Testament churches: 'Dear friends, do not believe every spirit, but test the spirits to see whether they are from God, because many false prophets have gone out into the world' (1 John 4:1).

If the LORD Jesus were physically present in our meetings, we would be awestruck. The speaker would immediately stop speaking, and we would fall on our faces in wonder and terrified love, as John did in Revelation 1:17. It would not be at all a light thing. But one thing would be very clear: we would know who was in charge. If a case was too difficult, we would know where to take it. If a question was puzzling, we would know who could answer it. When we needed a lead, we would know who should give it. We would know where to turn to distinguish good from evil, right from wrong, and wisdom from folly. We would know who was in charge.

But he's not here. And nor are his apostles. They too are gone. So although the promissory and revelatory function of the prophets has been fulfilled, the proclamatory function must necessarily continue. And although the foundational work of the apostles is given to us in scripture, which is the written testimony of their teaching, we still need preachers.

(c) ... and so we need preachers to continue the proclamatory work of the prophets

As with Israel after Moses, so with us after the apostolic age: we too have a written covenant document. Theirs was foundational but incomplete. Ours is full, sufficient and final, the canon of scripture. The prophets added to theirs; no preacher adds to ours. But just as they needed living prophets to preach the covenant, so we need living preachers to proclaim the word. As

Luther puts it, 'The Gospel is not really a document, but wishes to be a spoken word… That is why it must not be described with the pen but with the mouth…'[22]

The apostles commissioned successors like Timothy and Titus, and told them to commission others (2 Tim. 2:2), and to preach the word (2 Tim. 4:2). In this sense therefore the preacher's ministry is prophetic: it is not revelatory, but it is proclamatory. Indeed, the phrase 'man of God' in 1 Timothy 6:11 and 2 Timothy 3:17 echoes the same phrase in the Old Testament meaning a prophet.[23] Commenting on Romans 1:15, where Paul the letter-writer says he is 'eager to *preach* the gospel also to you who are at Rome', Haddon Robinson makes the point that even though the letter to the Romans is so magisterial, nevertheless Paul knew it was no substitute for preaching to them face to face (Rom. 1:15): 'That is why I am so eager to preach the gospel also to you who are at Rome.' He knows he cannot preach by a letter. Haddon Robinson comments that, 'A power comes through the word preached that even the inerrant written word cannot replace'.[24]

The New Testament recognises the strong parallels between prophets and preachers, not least in the negative parallels between false prophets and false teachers. For example in 2 Peter 2:1, 'There were also false prophets among the people, *just as* there will be false teachers among you' (cf. 1 John 4:1). This parallel is why William Perkins entitled his book about preaching, 'The Art of Prophesying'[25], and why some Puritan preaching meetings were called 'prophesyings'. They were affirming the continuation of the preaching role of the prophets even after their revelatory role had ceased.

So while the written scriptures provide the logical authority by which God governs Christ's church, it is preaching which

---

22. quoted in Peter Adam, *Speaking God's Words: a practical theology of preaching* (IVP, 1996) p. 114

23. John Woodhouse, *1 Samuel: Looking for a Leader* (Crossway Books, 2008), p. 562 n1

24. Haddon W. Robinson *Expository Preaching: Principles and Practice* (IVP, 1980), p. 17

25. William Perkins, *The Art of Prophesying* (1592. Banner of Truth Trust, 1982)

provides the practical authority. If we believe in the logical authority of the written word, we need to believe also in the practical primacy of the preached word.

An implication: Preaching promotes a proper attitude of submission to the Word of God

Listening to the preached word means *listening* and cannot just be transmuted into reading. Under the old covenant they submitted to God by listening to the prophet. Under the new covenant we submit to Christ by listening to Christ's preachers. It is by listening that we model submission.

Submission is not the same as discussion. Discussion is comfortably in line with the spirit of the age. We are happy to discuss and interpret. In a recent interview Rabbi Lionel Blue describes himself as 'a religious free-ranger, not a battery believer'. It is a clever metaphor: who would want to be cooped up in the confinement of fixed religious truth imposed on you by an external text or authoritative preaching, when you can range free, going where you want as an autonomous reader, creating your own meaning as you see fit? It conjures up images, on the one hand, of happy liberated people like him, contrasted with cooped-up cramped thinkers who believe some fixed body of doctrine.[26]

We live in a culture where everyone has their say, where I can press the interactive buttons and register my view on television, where I can set up a blog and proclaim my views on anything and everything to the world, where the most friendly thing we can say in welcoming newcomers is, 'We want to know what you think.' But – dare I say it – God does not want to know what we think. He wants us to know what he thinks.

The Danish theologian Søren Kierkegaard tells the parable of the King's Decree.[27] A King issues a decree. But instead of doing what the King says, his people begin to interpret it. One person publishes an interpretation. Then another. Every

---

26. *Oxford Today: the university magazine*, Vol.20, no.3 (Trinity 2008) p. 37
27. Søren Kierkegaard, *For Self-Examination: Recommended for the Times* (tr. Edna and Howard Yong. Minneapolis: Augsburg, 1940), p. 36, quoted in Kevin Vanhoozer *Is there a meaning in this text?* (IVP Apollos, 1998), p. 16

day new interpretations are broadcast: 'I think this is what the King meant'; 'I think that'; 'Well, anyway, we don't need to do anything about it.' And so no-one acts so as to do what the King commands.

Now clearly we cannot avoid interpretation. And there is a place for discussion and questioning to clarify our grasp of meaning and to correct one another's blind spots. But all too often, discussion is one of the ways we avoid submission. We need preaching with authority that we may listen submissively. This is counter-cultural. Perhaps it always has been. Back in 1907 P. T. Forsyth lamented, 'It is the absence of the note of authority that is the central weakness of so many of the churches.'[28] Paul writes to Titus (who was a preacher but not an apostle), 'These, then, are the things you should teach. Encourage and rebuke with all authority. Do not let anyone despise you (i.e. disregard what you say)' (Titus 2:15). It is in preaching that the authority of Christ is most clearly experienced. As P. T. Forsyth put it, 'The pulpit has an authority. If it have not, it is but a chair and not a pulpit. It may discourse, but it does not preach. But preach it must. It speaks with authority.'[29]

When the defining engagement of a church with the word of God is sitting together under preaching, all the other ministries of the word flourish. In all the other contexts in which we teach and admonish one another and speak the word of Christ to one another (Col. 3:16), we are much more likely to submit and not evade by endless discussion, if we have as our top meeting priority (alongside prayer) sitting together under the preached word.

But it doesn't easily work the other way round. A friend told me of someone who belongs to a supposedly evangelical church, but in which preaching has been effectively dethroned by what they call 'worship' (by which they mean corporate sung worship). This believer belongs to a house group. And she tries so hard to get the other members to pay attention to what the

28. P.T. Forsyth, *Positive Preaching and the Modern Mind* (3rd Edition. London: Independent Press, 1949), p. 27
29. ibid. p. 29

Bible says. But they won't. This is not surprising, really, when they see the Bible marginalised in the main Sunday meetings. And so of course they marginalise it in small meetings.

So let us preach with authority and listen with submissiveness.

We must end this chapter with a truth which functions as a necessary corrective against misunderstanding what I have said so far.

B. THE PREACHER'S AUTHORITY IS A BORROWED AUTHORITY, ONLY OBTAINED BY MUCH TOIL, SWEAT, AND WITH DEEP HUMBLING

Our first truth, that the preacher exercises the authority of Christ in the church, could be taken as a manifesto for preacherly aggrandisement. Look at me, says the big-headed preacher, I can speak the very words of God! So you may feel that this emphasis puffs up the preacher in a dangerous way and opens the way to a tyrannical authoritarianism among preachers. You may fear that this is not really about divine authority but rather opens the floodgates to human authoritarianism. Well, that can happen.

But I want to close this chapter by saying that those who seriously think this have not understood the nature of the preacher's authority. In the sixteenth century some of Calvin's opponents from the Church of Rome seem to have suggested that the authority of the Bible is borrowed from the authority of the church (since the church decided which books should be included). On the contrary, argued Calvin, scripture is the foundation of the church (Eph. 2:20) and the authority of the church's preachers is borrowed from its source, which is scripture.[30] Authority does not reside in the preacher as an individual, or in the preacher's office, or in his ordination or commissioning, or in his church as an institution. It resides in the written word of God. The source of authority is Christ. The locus of authority is the Bible, in its entirety. So I am not advocating the Barthian view that parts of the Bible *become* the word of God from time to time

---

30. T.H.L. Parker, *Calvin's Preaching* ((T & T Clark, 1992), p. 3

as they are preached. No, the Bible 'is like a royal sceptre' and we must not imagine that the Kingdom of Christ exists 'apart from his sceptre (that is, his most holy Word).'[31]

Nevertheless the usual instrument by which God wields this authority is the preacher. So the question is this: is the preached word also the word of God? The Bible is the word of God; but can the sermon be the word of God? The answer must be: 'Sometimes'. Clearly it isn't always, for there are false teachers. But it is sometimes, since Peter says to those who speak (in the context of local church ministries) that they should do so, as those who speak 'the very words of God' (1 Pet. 4:11). So it must be possible, otherwise it would be perverse of Peter to exhort us to do it.

So what is the relationship between the written word and the preached word? 'The preaching of the Word of God is the Word of God' wrote the Second Helvetic Confession in 1566.[32] And that certainly begs a few questions! When the Reformer Bullinger addressed this issue, he began by dismissing two mistakes.[33] On the one hand, the Roman church said that scripture was not clear and needed an interpretive key from outside. But scripture is not in need of a key brought from outside, whether it is the church's magisterium or the interpretive consensus of the scholarly guild, or whatever. It is not like some locked door for which we must search outside for the key. It is not a cryptic or coded document.

On the other hand, some radicals said that scripture was so clear that it was sufficient just to read it, and there was no need of exposition (and most certainly no need to train preachers). All we need, they said, is the public reading of scripture; expository preachers are surplus to requirements. But, as Bullinger pointed out, although scripture is clear, it does not wear its clarity on its sleeve.

---

31. Calvin, *Institutes* 3.xx.42
32. quoted in Peter Adam, *Speaking God's Words* (IVP, 1996), p. 112
33. T.H.L. Parker, *Calvin's Preaching* (Edinburgh: T&T Clark, 1992) chapter 3

The Authority of the Preached Word

There is a theological reason for this, which is worth exploring. What is the purpose of scripture? It is to make men and women wise for salvation through faith in Jesus Christ (2 Tim. 3:15) and thereby to transform them into the likeness of Christ. And because scripture is in the business of transforming people, it needs to be preached by people who are themselves being transformed by scripture. Moses didn't just preach the covenant; the covenant gripped him. He was a kind of embodied covenant person.

And therefore there are no shortcuts to preaching with authority. This authority is a wonderful authority, but it is an authority borrowed only at great cost. This is why there are no shortcuts that work. I conclude with three warnings about shortcuts which we preachers may be tempted to take.

1. *Beware the shortcut of individual interpretation*

This is the idea that I, in my study, can just beaver away and interpret the scripture on my own, as if I were the first person to whom the word of God had come. But no, the preacher cannot by-pass accountability to others, both living and dead. We are not bound to submit to the interpretations of other Christians, whether our contemporaries or our predecessors, but we are bound in humility to listen to them. We must not be lazily idiosyncratic. We need the hard work of listening to one another, not least to allow others to show us our cultural blind-spots.

2. *Beware the shortcut of second-hand interpretation*

Beware the idea that a quick Google will come up with good sermon material, or that listening to recordings of other preachers will enable us to put together a passable sermon quickly. The internet is a dangerous place when we think it is a panacea for quick preparation.

I still shiver to remember a talk I gave as a young speaker at a school Christian Union. I had heard a brilliant talk on the same passage (it was the Good Shepherd passage in John 10) given in a different context by a famous preacher. It was so good, and I was convinced I could not hope to do better, so – and I am ashamed to admit this – I actually typed it out and delivered the same talk. It sank like a lead balloon, for two reasons. Firstly, the context in which I was speaking was different from the context in which the original exposition had been given. But secondly – and this is my point here – by copying someone else's exposition I failed lamentably to grapple with the passage myself in such a way that the passage got into my bloodstream. And so when I spoke there was not only a discontinuity of context (a different audience) and style (the famous preacher's rather than mine), but there was also a terrible superficiality in my speaking. I spoke from my script but not from my heart. My heart had not been shaped and changed by the passage through hours of personal grappling. I shall never make that mistake again. The experience has left me with a great reluctance to listen to recordings of other preachers preaching a passage I am preparing, at least until I have first worked, puzzled, prayed and grappled at length with the passage myself.

3. *Beware the shortcut of mystical authority*

There is no mystical short-cut, whereby the lazy preacher can hope to be clothed by some anointing, so that his ill-prepared words will come with the power of God. We may want to claim the promise of Psalm 81:10, where God says, 'Open wide your mouth and I will fill it!' If we open wide our mouths having not bothered to prepare, he will indeed fill them; but, as someone has said, he will fill them with hot air! (And of course Psalm 81:10 is not about preaching, so we are twisting the meaning of the verse anyway.) We need desperately the fresh filling of God's Holy Spirit when we preach, and can accomplish nothing without his sovereign power; but that power does not in general come upon preachers who have not bothered to prepare, and the filling of the Spirit is not a God-given compensation for wilful idleness.

The Authority of the Preached Word

Calvin wrote, 'If I should climb up into the pulpit without having deigned to look at a book and frivolously imagine, "Ah well! When I get there God will give me enough to talk about," and I do not condescend to read, or to think about what I ought to declare, and I come here without carefully pondering how I must apply the Holy Scripture to the edification of the people – well, then I should be a cock-sure charlatan and God would put me to confusion in my audaciousness.'[34]

Implication: Persevere in costly expository ministry
The whole point of borrowed authority is that I must constantly have recourse to the source. This is why authoritative expository preaching is no light task, and why preachers need to be set apart to devote themselves to the apostolic work of prayer and the ministry of the word (Acts 6:4) and to persevere in that ministry.

In one sense, it is perfectly true that every Christian can prophesy (Acts 2:17ff). We may all speak to others for their upbuilding, encouragement and consolation (1 Cor. 14:3). As the word of Christ dwells in a church richly we teach and admonish one another (Col. 3:16). But not too many should be teachers (James 3:1); some are gifted and set apart to be pastors and teachers (Eph. 4:11), and they are set free to labour at preaching and teaching (1 Tim. 5:17). They need to be set free to devote themselves to this, because it is a very demanding work. It takes time, prayer, sweat, wrestling, pain, puzzling, hard thinking and perseverance. This is why expository preaching is as necessary now as it was in any age.

Expository preaching lets God set the agenda, as we open up the written word in the order, the form, and the books which he has chosen to give us. We do not make the staple diet of our preaching just dotting around with miscellaneous passages in the Lectionary, or preaching topics of our choice, or preaching our systematic theology or what we feel a church needs; by making expository preaching the staple diet, we let God set the agenda.[35]

---

34. Sermon on Deuteronomy 6:16, quoted in T.H.L. Parker, *Calvin's Preaching* (T & T Clark, 1992), p.. 81
35. See the Appendix for this point developed

The Priority of Preaching

We persevere in the hard discipline of immersing ourselves in a Bible book for a preaching series, so that the word gets right into the preacher as the preacher gets into the word. We wrestle and struggle with the word. As a preacher friend of mine put it, we lay ourselves on the anvil and come out of our preparation and our preaching hurting, as our own sin is exposed; we ourselves are moved afresh to repentance and faith, as we feel the pain of a rebellious, dying world. This is what happens as we let a book of the Bible sink deep into us and we immerse ourselves in it. Those who just relish quiet time in the study and think preparation is an enjoyable experience have missed the point; there is a kind of study and preparation that can just be self-indulgent. Year after year I grieve at how slow, how dim, how spiritually obtuse I am, and therefore how long it takes for God to get his word through my calloused skin and deep into my heart. Godly preparation is a struggle, but there is no substitute for the time and the pain of this engagement with the word.

And yet, as we struggle with the word, we begin to speak with all the varied tones of voice of the Scripture, with freshness and variety; there will be nothing predictable or banal, no flat dull faithfulness about our preaching. There are no mystical shortcuts, no second-hand shortcuts, no individualistic shortcuts.

Those who think this doctrine of authority puffs up the preacher have not begun to feel the sheer terror of being a preacher. They think preachers want to be in the pulpit. Well, some do. But no preacher who wants to be in the pulpit ought to be in the pulpit. Nobody who likes the limelight ought to be a preacher. We do not want in our pulpits men like Diotrephes who loved to have the pre-eminence, who couldn't wait to be given the microphone (3 John 9). No, to be a preacher is one of the most deeply humbling experiences in the world. Preaching drives us to our knees, puts gigantic butterflies in our stomachs, and makes us cry out, 'Who is sufficient for these things?'

This borrowed authority is costly. But what a prize there is to be won! As Calvin put it, the reason a man climbs into the pulpit is, 'that God may speak to us by the mouth of a man.'[36] John Jewel, Bishop of Salisbury from 1522 to 1572, wrote this: 'Despise not, good brethren, despise not to hear God's Word declared. As you tender your own souls, be diligent to come to sermons; for that is the ordinary place where men's hearts be moved, and God's secrets be revealed. For, *be the preacher never so weak*, yet is the Word of God as mighty and puissant as ever it was.'[37]

As William Sangster put it, there can be no substitute 'for a Spirit-filled man looking men in the face and speaking the word of God to their consciences and hearts.'[38] This ought to be a great encouragement to us as we prepare for Sunday. To the discouraged leader we should say, 'There is no one who can bring the word of God to *this* flock this Sunday as you *uniquely* are in a position to do.' To preach in this gathering of the local church is an awesome privilege. As we listen to you, we listen to him.

---

36. T.H.L. Parker, *Calvin's Preaching* (Edinburgh: T&T Clark, 1992), p. 24
37. Works of John Jewel Vol.II, p. 1034, quoted in John R.W. Stott, *I believe in Preaching* (Hodder and Stoughton, 1962), p. 119 (emphasis mine)
38. W.E. Sangster, *The Craft of the Sermon* (London: Epworth Press, 1954), p. 11

2

Preaching that Transforms the Church

Deuteronomy 30:11-20

[11]Now what I am commanding you today is not too difficult for you or beyond your reach. [12]It is not up in heaven, so that you have to ask, "Who will ascend into heaven to get it and proclaim it to us so we may obey it?" [13]Nor is it beyond the sea, so that you have to ask, "Who will cross the sea to get it and proclaim it to us so we may obey it?" [14]No, the word is very near you; it is in your mouth and in your heart so that you may obey it.

[15]See, I set before you today life and prosperity, death and destruction. [16]For I command you today to love the LORD your God, to walk in his ways, and to keep his commands, decrees and laws; then you will live and increase, and the LORD your God will bless you in the land you are entering to possess.

[17]But if your heart turns away and you are not obedient, and if you are drawn away to bow down to other gods and worship them, [18]I declare to you this day that you will certainly be destroyed. You will not live long in the land you are crossing the Jordan to enter and possess.

[19]This day I call heaven and earth as witnesses against you that I have set before you life and death, blessings and curses. Now choose life, so that you and your children may live [20]and that you may love the LORD your God, listen to his voice, and hold fast to him. For the LORD is your life, and he will give you many years in the land he swore to give to your fathers, Abraham, Isaac and Jacob.

PREACHING THAT GRIPS

'Therefore choose life' (Deut. 30:19). Compressed in those three words lies a lifetime of passionate transformative preaching. Deuteronomy 30:11-20 is the closing section of the last sermon preached by Israel's first and greatest Old Testament preacher. Moses preaches as a dying man to an Israel who will enter the land without him. And he knows it.

Moses' sermon is riveting. It grips our attention and commands our hearts. The subject of this second chapter is preaching that transforms the church, God's people transformed by the preached word of God.

The trouble is, all of us who are preachers know only too painfully what it is both to hear and to preach the very opposite of riveting transformative sermons. One of my favourite comic cameos is from Charles Dickens' great novel *David Copperfield*. The young David describes a sermon in church, and how their pew has a window near it, 'out of which our house can be seen, and *is* seen many times during the morning's service, by Peggotty (the maid), who likes to make herself as sure as she can that it's not being robbed, or is not in flames. But though Peggotty's eye wanders, she is much offended if mine does, and frowns to me, as I stand upon the seat, that I am to look at the clergyman. But I can't always look at him ... I am afraid of his wondering why I stare so, and perhaps stopping the service to enquire – and what am I to do?' He looks at his mother, who pretends not to see him. He looks at the boy across the aisle, but he makes faces back. 'I look at the sunlight coming in at the open door through the porch, and there I see a stray sheep –

Preaching that Transforms the Church

I don't mean a sinner, but mutton – half making up his mind to come into the church … I look up at the monumental tablets on the wall, and try to think of Mr Bodgers late of this parish, and what the feelings of Mrs Bodgers must have been, when affliction sore, long time he bore, and physicians were in vain. I wonder whether they called in Mr Chillip (their family doctor) and he was in vain; and if so, how he likes to be reminded of it once a week.[1] And so it goes on. Most preachers know the sinking feeling of preaching and being acutely aware that there are people in front of us just like that, disengaged and inattentive, their minds a million miles away from the word of God.

In chapter one we considered the authority of the expository preacher as he speaks the very words of God. We took as our starting point Moses the prototypical prophet and considered that great line of preaching prophets through the Old Testament, continuing into the New Testament as proclaimers of the new covenant in Jesus Christ. Our theme was authority, that the preacher can speak the very words of God, that Christ exercises his authority over his church not by the written word, but by the written word preached. We ended by making the point that the preacher's authority is a borrowed authority, borrowed only through great toil and pain. Expository ministry that has the authority of God keeps the preacher on his knees.

In this chapter we will consider Moses in Deuteronomy as a model of preaching that transforms, proclamation that grips, an opening up of the word of God in a way that engages, and that has about it an engaged clear passionate urgency offering Christ to men and women. We saw in chapter one how Deuteronomy is God's mandate for the preaching of the covenant by the prophet like Moses. Moses' preaching is a model for us of how preaching ought to be. Moses the prototypical prophet is also the prototypical preacher. I suspect the preacher in *David Copperfield* was not preaching as Moses preached.

---

1.   Charles Dickens, *David Copperfield* (1850. Penguin Classics edition, 2004), p. 27

We will consider the difference between preaching and merely teaching the Bible. My reason for focussing on this is that I think it may be a necessary corrective to an imbalance in some of our circles. For some time we have emphasised the centrality of 'teaching the Bible' in pastoral ministry. That was good because it stopped us being side-tracked onto teaching our systematic theology or our experience, or just setting out strategic thinking or baptising the wisdom of the world with a religious veneer. We were reminded that we were leading our churches by teaching *the Bible*. But I fear that we have so emphasised 'teaching *the Bible*' that we rest happy with '*teaching* the Bible'. But preaching the Bible is more than teaching the Bible, let alone simply explaining the Bible. Many of us have been introduced as a visiting speaker with the words, 'Now so and so will explain the Bible/teach the Bible.' When that happens to me I want to interrupt and say, 'Yes, I hope to explain and teach it. But I hope also to preach it, and that is not the same.'

We are going to consider four preaching themes in Deuteronomy, all of which feature in Deuteronomy 30:11-20, although we shall also look elsewhere:

1. The reality of God
2. The stubbornness of people
3. The urgency of faith
4. The wonder of grace

THEME 1. THE REALITY OF GOD
'See, I set before you today life and prosperity, death and destruction' (Deut. 30:15). Moses says that if you obey the commandments of the LORD your God – that is, if you are believers, justified by faith, loving him, walking with him, keeping faith with him – then you will live. Otherwise you will die. You cannot avoid that choice, because God alone is real; he is Truth with a capital 'T'.

Moses preaches under an awesome sense of the transcendent reality of God. In Deuteronomy 4:24 he preaches to them that 'the LORD your God is a consuming fire, a jealous God.' If you are with him, his fire will consume all your enemies (Deut. 9:3 'the LORD your God is the one who goes across ahead of you like a devouring fire'); your enemies will be his enemies, and he will eat up and destroy everything in his path. But the flip side of that is that if you are not with him, if you are unfaithful, disloyal, then he will consume you. You will place yourself in the path of consuming fire. So when unconverted people hear the voice of God at Sinai they can't stand it and cry that, 'this great fire will consume us' and that they need a mediator (Deut. 5:25). He 'is the faithful God, keeping his covenant of love to a thousand generations of those who love him and keep his commands. But those who hate him he will repay to their face by destruction; he will not be slow to repay to their face those who hate him. Therefore take care…' (Deut. 7:9-11).

He is 'a jealous God', a fiercely jealous husband who will not share his wife's affections with another. He is the all or nothing God. 'The LORD our God, the LORD is *one*' (6:4). He is not simply the only God who exists; he is the one defining reality of the universe. This hasn't changed. When Hebrews 12 speaks of the new covenant the writer concludes by quoting Deuteronomy 4:24, 'our God is a consuming fire' (Heb. 12:29).

When Moses says this, he is not being arbitrary; this is not a power-play, a threat designed to recruit more people to the religion he and his mates have made up. This is reality. This awesome God is real; he is the Creator, and therefore this is how the world is. This is not a marketing ploy to get people into our religion; this is how the world is. This is not part of a comparative religion competition, weighing up the pros and cons of different religions to see which we will vote out of the Big Religion house. This is reality. Human beings cannot change it. Moses preaches with a deep pervading sense of this unavoidable reality. God is a consuming fire. I set before you life and death. You cannot make the wrong choice and still get life. If you line yourself up with this God, reality is on your side; if you set yourself up against him, you have reality against you.

In chapter one I quoted from a recent interview with Rabbi Lionel Blue in which he describes himself as 'a religious free-ranger, not a battery believer'. Nevertheless, he admits that this is a personal choice, which works for him, not a final description of ultimate reality. 'For someone else,' he says, 'I can quite see that spirituality might lie in the beauty of an equation.'[2] How wrong he is.

We live in a culture that has left reality behind, even in surprising places. We might think the journal *The Economist* is a sober publication, with its feet on the ground. But in 2008 it carried an obituary of the Maharishi Mahesh Yogi, the one-time mentor of the Beatles and proponent of Transcendental Meditation. It was a very positive obituary. What a good person he was, they said, and what noble aims he had for world peace. His message 'was entirely laudable'. Never mind that he believed in 'yogic flying'. At least he didn't 'promote ... a mainstream religion preaching original sin... and the likelihood of eternal damnation.'[3] Never mind reality. Never mind the absurdity of yogic flying. At least we liked his message. In writing like this they have left reality behind.

In his brilliant evangelistic book *Real Life Jesus* Mike Cain gives this illustration for people who say, 'Well, Christianity is fine for you. But I'm just not the religious type.' Imagine you and I are by the Clifton Suspension Bridge in Bristol, 80 metres above the Avon Gorge. You decide to walk down to the towpath. As you start, I stay behind and begin to climb over the railings. As I am about to step out into mid-air you yell, 'Mike, what are you doing? You'll kill yourself.' 'No, not me,' I reply, 'You see, I'm not the gravity type.' But gravity is not a lifestyle choice; gravity is reality. The God who is consuming fire is reality; whether you or I believe it makes no difference to reality, but it will make an eternity of difference to us.[4]

This awesome sense of God means that Moses applies the reality of God to the vagaries of culture. His preaching

---

2.   *Oxford Today: the university magazine*, Vol.20, no.3 (Trinity 2008) p. 37

3.   *The Economist* February 16th 2008, p. 99

4.   Mike Cain, *Real Life Jesus* (IVP, 2008) pp. 25, 26

is engaged with the world because the God he preaches is the Creator of the world and not some little godlet of the ghetto.

It is important to stress this engagement with reality. Melvin Tinker has warned of expository preaching in which 'there is no serious engagement with …culture' so that, 'many evangelical sermons may be sound, but have no cutting edge for the simple reason there is no real engagement taking place between the Word and the world. The problem with liberalism is that it has sold out to the world; the problem with pietistic evangelicalism is that it retreats from the world, shouting at it from a distance or simply ignoring it'.[5] Liberalism claims to permeate and influence culture, but only does so in the way that a mouse permeates a cat; it is swallowed by it. But some evangelicalism so withdraws from culture that our preaching fails to engage.

Moses, by contrast, understands the culture of Egypt (from which they have come) and the culture of Canaan (to which they are going). He knows about the seductions of money, sex and power in Egypt (which is why he warns the King against them in Deut. 17:14-20). He knows about the sexy Asherim and the virile Baals in Canaan. He has read their prospectuses; he sees their advertisements. He knows what they offer. He has seen how they are worshipped. He understands their prosperity gospel. He knows they too promise 'life and good', and all sorts of very real bodily blessings, but they cannot perform what they promise. And so in his preaching Moses engages with the culture surrounding the people to whom he preaches.

Kevin Vanhoozer has made the point that if we love our neighbour we must learn to understand his culture: 'cultural literacy … is … an integral aspect of obeying the law of love.'[6] Preaching that engages with culture will press home on people that reality is on our side. We are not canvassing their vote,

---

5.   Melvin Tinker, 'Engaging with Liberalism' *Churchman* 122/1 (Spring 2008), p. 57

6.   Kevin Vanhoozer et al (eds) *Everyday Theology: How to Read Cultural Texts and Interpret Trends* (Baker Academic, 2007), p. 19

but pleading with them to live in line with how the world is. The Creator God is a consuming fire. The only way to have reality on our side is to have him on our side, which is what the gospel offers. We must preach as Moses did with this awesome awareness of the reality of the God we proclaim.

THEME 2. THE STUBBORNNESS OF PEOPLE

'But if your heart turns away and you are not obedient (ESV 'will not hear'), and if you are drawn away to bow down to other gods and worship them…' (Deut. 30:17).

Their hearts will turn away, and Moses knows this. One of the things that makes Moses such a powerful preacher is that he is never misled by a warm smile. He knows the human heart. That is one of the great things John said about the LORD Jesus, that 'he knew what was in a man' (John 2:25). I don't know about you, but I am so easily misled by externalism. The men and women in front of me look so pleasant, so friendly (sometimes), so religious, so respectable, so sweetly reasonable. If there is anything wrong with them, I'm sure it is nothing that a quiet cup of tea and a chat by the fireside won't put right. And so I find myself slipping into what has been called the Socratic fallacy, that if I persuade them with rational argument (like Socrates), if I get my arguments clear and educate them, then education will change them. If I teach them the Bible, they'll get it.

I ought to know better, because I ought to know my own heart. Moses understands their hearts. Again and again in his preaching he anticipates their reactions: 'Do not say to yourself …' 'Do not say in your heart …' 'Beware lest you say …' – because he knows that this is exactly what they will say.

Moses understands their unbelieving fears. 'You may say to yourselves, "These nations are stronger than we are. How can we drive them out?"' (Deut. 7:17). He says 'you may say' because he knows their unbelieving hearts; they will indeed say this, and Moses anticipates it.

Moses understands their pride. 'You may say to yourself, "My power and the strength of my hands have produced this wealth for me.'" (Deut. 8:17). He says 'you may say' because he knows their pride; this is exactly what they will say, and Moses once again anticipates it.

Above all, Moses understands their stubbornness. In chapters 1-3, as he retells the story of the desert journeys, he presses home their stubborn guilt. For example, 'In spite of this (i.e. in spite of the words of reassurance and grace they have received) you did not trust in the LORD your God' (Deut.1:32). God spoke words of grace with great force and clarity, but they simply didn't believe him.

Most forcefully in Deuteronomy 9:4-24 he preaches to them the sin of their hearts. 'Do not say in your heart, after the LORD your God has thrust them out before you, "It is because of my righteousness that the LORD has brought me in …" But it is not because of your righteousness or the uprightness of your heart… you are a stubborn people' (Deut.9:4ff. ESV). Moses reminds them at some length that he had hardly disappeared from sight up Mt. Sinai before they turned aside ('quickly' Deut. 9:16) and made God furiously angry by their stubborn hearts. And in Deut.9:22 he slips in, 'By the way, I can think of lots of other occasions when you proved yourselves the same.' The golden calf was not atypical, but prototypical of human behaviour. In summary, 'You have been rebellious against the LORD ever since I have known you' (Deut. 9:24).

Stephen echoes Moses: 'You stiff-necked people, with uncircumcised hearts and ears! You are just like your fathers: You always resist the Holy Spirit!' (Acts 7:51). Like Moses, and like Stephen, we must be realistic and never be misled into thinking that just because people are religious they are good-hearted. We are not, and nor are they.

Application: Preaching that is silent dialogue
At this point I want to pause and talk about preaching which is neither monologue nor dialogue. I want to question the way we usually think about these two. I want to suggest that in some ways when two or more people speak it can still be monologue, and when only one person speaks it may have the character of

dialogue. Formally, of course, if only one person speaks it's a monologue; if more than one person speaks it's a dialogue. But in substance it may be paradoxically different.

The issue is engagement. Although in his preaching Moses is the only speaker, it would be misleading to call his preaching a monologue. So often this is the objection we face: 'There you are, six feet above contradiction, pulpiteering, setting yourself up as if you knew what to say, and expecting me to sit submissively while you rant on and on in your "monotonous ministerial monologue" or even "a monstrous monologue by a moron to mutes,"[7] "poor little talkative Christianity". And as you rant you show that you don't understand me at all, you don't know what I'm thinking, you've no insight into my doubts and fears, you are ignorant of my pressures or temptations, you don't know anything at all. You are just an ignorant preacher.' We say of someone rather full of himself, who pontificates in a conversation, 'I'm afraid he was rather preachy.' And so when we come to preach we are frightened of preaching lest we be thought preachy.

Sadly, sometimes it's true. There is preaching like that, which has all the drawbacks of a monologue and none of the qualities of authority. But this is not the preaching Moses models for us. Indeed we may say that Moses' preaching is one person speaking with the character of a public dialogue. Moses does not simply expound the covenant; he engages with his hearers.

John Stott speaks of 'the silent dialogue which should be developing between the preacher and his hearers. For what he says provokes questions in their minds which he then proceeds to answer. His answer raises further questions, to which again he replies. One of the greatest gifts a preacher needs is such a sensitive understanding of people and their problems that he can anticipate their reactions to each part of his sermon and respond to them'[8]. This is what Moses does.

---

7.   R.E.O. White, *A Guide to Preaching*, quoted in John R.W. Stott, *I believe in Preaching* (Hodder and Stoughton, 1962), p. 60

8.   John R.W. Stott, *I believe in Preaching* (Hodder and Stoughton, 1962), p. 61

But how do we answer those who say, 'Why settle for a silent dialogue? Why not have an actual spoken dialogue?' In their evangelistic ministries in Acts, the apostles seem to mix dialogue with preaching pretty much interchangeably.[9] Of course they do. They have little alternative with unconverted people. An unconverted person will only listen to me if I listen to him. Which is why I have not heard of a church inviting outsiders to an evangelistic 'Monologue Supper'! Of course we must engage in dialogue to win a hearing, as the apostles did.

But it is worth remembering that our aim is that we become less interested in the sounds of our own voices and more attentive to the voice of God. As we considered in chapter 1, we are to 'Listen to him!' The more deeply converted I am, the more appetite I will have to sit under the preached word, and the less concerned I will be to have the opportunity to participate in a dialogue, to get my word in edgeways, to make my views known and get myself heard.

What is more, the grass is not always greener on the dialogue side of the monologue/dialogue fence. There may be times when a silent dialogue in preaching is actually preferable to a spoken dialogue. Some so-called dialogue is really simultaneous or alternating monologue. Although formally the speeches made by Job and his comforters are a dialogue, it is really a dialogue of the deaf and might just as well be interleaved or alternating monologues.[10] Good spoken dialogue is easier said than done. How often a dialogue is hijacked by some over-talkative person asking questions that most of the others don't want answered! Sometimes a coherent reasoned exposition is interrupted by irrelevant questions. Spoken dialogue sounds good, and it is sometimes necessary, but there are both practical and theological reasons for working at the silent dialogue of good preaching.

---

9.   e.g. Acts 18:19; 19:8
10.   Christopher Ash, *Out of the Storm: grappling with God in the book of Job* (IVP, 2004), p. 43

But if we are to do silent dialogue well, our preaching must be built on a foundation of deep knowledge of people and therefore engagement with culture. John Owen writes, 'It is the duty of a shepherd to know the state of his flock…What probably are their principal temptations, their hindrances and furtherances, what is their growth and decay?' Otherwise our preaching will be "like a man beating of the air" with little chance of hitting a target.[11]

Richard Baxter agreed wholeheartedly with this priority of preaching. Although he is known best for his pastoral care of individuals and families, Baxter called preaching 'the most excellent' part of the ministry of the word, and preached for an hour most Thursdays and Sundays. But, as Baxter affirmed, we must know the people to whom we preach: '…it is necessary, that we should know our charge,' he wrote in *The Reformed Pastor*, 'for how can we take heed to them if we do not know them? We must labour to be acquainted, not only with the persons, but with the state of our people, with their inclinations and conversations; what are the sins of which they are most in danger – and what are the duties they are most apt to neglect, and what temptations are they most liable to; for if we know not their temperament or disease, we are not likely to prove successful physicians.'[12]

I do not think this means that every preacher has to become a great cultural expert. It can be daunting to hear a speaker imply that unless we all become equipped to give deep and perceptive analyses of everything from the fashion industry to climate change, we cannot preach. We cannot each become experts in every aspect of our culture and contemporary issues. What we can and must do is to love the people we serve and the people we seek to reach. And if we love people we will listen to them and begin to understand them. And if we do that thoughtfully we are bound to get insight into culture.

---

11. *The Works of John Owen*, vol.4, p. 510 f. (Edinburgh: Banner of Truth, 1967), quoted in Peter Adam, *Speaking God's Words: a practical theology of preaching* (IVP, 1996) p. 159
12. Richard Baxter, *The Reformed Pastor* (1656. Banner of Truth Trust, 1989), p. 90

I still remember with some frustration the first sermon series I preached after immersing myself in my theology degree studies. The studies were worthwhile and I gained a lot from them. But when I went straight from this academic immersion into a summer pulpit series, I struggled to pray myself into the shoes of my hearers. I was preaching Colossians, and I like to think I expounded Colossians better than I would have done before my theological studies. But I earthed my preaching in realistic engagement with my hearers much less well. That engagement comes only from week by week time with people.

This has implications for the size of churches. It places a question mark over the ambition of church leaders to see their churches grow and grow, and suggests that planting new churches or reinvigorating smaller existing churches may reap relational dividends in terms of how well those with pastoral oversight can know their people. There are obvious reasons why we may prefer large churches; but it is more relational to preach to a church small enough for you to know its members, and for them to know you.

So after our first two themes we see that Moses preaches with an awesome sense of the reality of God and a sober realism about the stubbornness of the human heart. He therefore engages in a silent dialogue with his hearers. This is preaching that engages.

THEME 3. THE URGENCY OF FAITH

Moses understands that faith is always the response of today and never the response of yesterday. 'Today' or 'this day' is one of the great themes in Moses' preaching (for example, Deut. 30:15, 16, 18, 19). To have 'many years' (ESV 'length of days') in the land (Deut. 30:20) depends upon the response of today. And the thing about today is that it is always today. This gives to Moses' preaching an existential urgency. Every time he preaches it is today; and he calls for response today. Gordon McConville brilliantly traces this theme in his commentary on

Deuteronomy,[13] how Israel are to enter covenant today and then today and again today, as long as it is called today.

Let's trace some of this theme. In chapter one Moses reminds them there was a day when the LORD set the land before the people (Deut. 1:21). He set before them life and good, death and evil. They chose death and died in the wilderness. Then at the start of chapter 4 he reminds them of another 'today', at Baal-Peor on the edge of the land (Num. 25). Again, they faced a choice. Some chose death, and they died. But 'all of you who held fast to the LORD your God are still alive today' (Deut. 4:4). So what does he say to them? Does he say, 'Well done, choosing life yesterday. Rest on your laurels.'? Not at all. He ends that sermon with the rousing challenge: 'Acknowledge and take to heart this day that the LORD is God in heaven above and on the earth below. There is no other ...' So be faithful to him today (Deut. 4:39, 40).

Then at the start of chapter 5 he says, 'Hear, O Israel.... The LORD our God made a covenant with *us* at Horeb. It was not with our fathers that the LORD made this covenant, but with us, with all of *us* who are alive here today. The LORD spoke to *you* face to face out of the fire on the mountain' (Deut. 5:1-4). The covenant is brought into the present by the existential urgency of Moses' preaching 'today', on that later day. And that is the model for urgent preaching every day that is called today. The scriptures that were not originally written to us were nonetheless written for us who are alive today.

The theme continues in chapter 26, the ceremony of the firstfruits. They are to come to the priest who is in office at the time (Deut. 26:3). This envisages a later 'today', indeed a succession of later 'todays' in the land. On that later 'today' they are to say to the priest, 'I declare today to the LORD your God that I have come to the land that the LORD swore to our forefathers to give us.' To say, 'I have come to the land' is not a geographical statement; it's not something you could read off your SatNav. It's a theological

---

13. J.G. McConville, *Deuteronomy* (IVP Apollos Old Testament Commentary, 2002)

statement: 'I'm a believer, I trust the God of promise, who gave us this land.' And you said it year after year. You don't present your first-fruits and say, 'I came into the land twenty years ago, and here's my testimony written out, that I've fished out of the top drawer of my desk.' No, you say, 'I declare today that I have come to the land.' We see it again in Deuteronomy 26:16-19 ('You have declared *this day* that the LORD is your God … And the LORD has declared *this day* that you are his people, his treasured possession …'). This is covenant renewal so long as it is called today. We see this immediacy again in Deuteronomy 27:9, when Moses and the priests declare to all Israel, '…You have *now* (i.e. today) become the people of the LORD your God.'

It always is 'today'. In Lewis Carroll's *Through the Looking Glass,* the Red Queen says, 'jam tomorrow and jam yesterday, but never jam today'; and so it is never jam, for it is always today. The appeal for decision today runs right through Deuteronomy. Indeed, 'this preoccupation with exhortation is the most striking feature of the book's language.'[14]

The theme continues in the covenant renewal ceremony of Joshua 24: '…choose for yourselves *this day* whom you will serve' (Josh. 24:15). It's no use them saying, 'There's no need for all this crisis and challenge. You needn't worry about us. We chose yesterday.' The theological point is this: I may have chosen yesterday. But the litmus test of whether I really chose yesterday is that I will again make the same choice today. Otherwise the choice I say I made yesterday was a shallow and spurious choice and an empty profession of faith.

This 'today' theme of urgency is picked up in Psalm 95:7, 8 with its appeal, 'Today, if you hear his voice, do not harden your hearts …' And the writer to the Hebrews develops and preaches on it in Hebrews 3:7–4:13. We are to 'encourage (exhort) one another daily, as long as it is called Today, so that none of you may be hardened by sin's deceitfulness' (Heb. 3:13).

---

14.   J. Gary Millar, *Now Choose Life: Theology and Ethics in Deuteronomy* (IVP Apollos, 1998), p. 47

Paul has the same 'today' urgency to the Corinthians when he implores them to be reconciled to God, and to do so urgently because '*now* is the time of God's favour, *now* is the day of salvation' (2 Cor. 5:20-6:2).

Writing to believers in whom the word of Christ has already been implanted (they are regenerate), James doesn't tell them to relax; rather he exhorts them to 'get rid of all moral filth and the evil that is so prevalent, and humbly accept the word planted in you, which can save you' (James 1:21). The word has been implanted; but today and every day it must be received and accepted afresh with trusting obedience.

The 19th Century Cambridge Anglican evangelical minister Charles Simeon wrote a three brilliant pages on 'Directions how to hear sermons.'[15] Expounding the LORD's warning, 'Take heed therefore how ye hear' (Luke 8:18) he writes that our LORD's caution is important, 'Because every discourse increases either our salvation or condemnation. The word delivered is either a savour of life or of death.' (2 Cor. 2:15f.). So we must take heed today.

When we first repent and believe 'today', we do not then leave repentance and believing behind tomorrow. We do not file it away, put the response card in the top drawer. No, we enter a lifetime of daily repenting and believing. Tim Keller loves to remind us of the first of Luther's 95 theses at Wittenberg in 1517: 'When our LORD and Master Jesus Christ said, "Repent" (Matt 4:17), he willed the entire life of believers to be one of repentance.' And we might add, one of faith. Preaching calls us to this with existential urgency.

Commenting on the instruction to 'listen to him (the prophet)' in Deuteronomy 18, Calvin says, 'But, since it would be insufficient that they should be *once* instructed in the proper

---

15. My version is in *Let Wisdom Judge: University Addresses and Sermon Outlines by Charles Simeon* (Inter-Varsity Fellowship, 1959), p. 188ff. See also my contemporary reworking of Simeon, *Listen Up! A Practical Guide to Listening to Sermons* (Good Book Company, 2009)

worship of God by a written law, unless *daily preaching* were subjoined, God expressly furnishes his prophets with authority ...'[16] We need repeated preaching, because by nature we will never repent and believe. We will 'move on' from the simple gospel of daily repentance, daily taking up the cross, daily faith, to a supposed higher life, a more sophisticated life, some kind of super-spiritual life in which repentance and faith are too ordinary and simple to be practised. This is what will happen unless we sit under faithful preaching. We need the urgency of a city watchman to cry out, 'Listen to the sound of the trumpet!' (Jer. 6:17).

Application: urgent passionate clarity

The urgency of faith means we need to preach with urgent passionate clarity, clear urgent passion, and passionate clear urgency. Let's take those three, clarity, urgency and passion, and apply them to our preaching.

(a) Clarity

Moses is so clear. People criticise Deuteronomy for its repetitive style, but Moses knows he must be clear; and if some aesthetes don't like the style, so much the worse for them.

Moses knows that there are hidden things we do not need to know; but there are also revealed things, things we need to know, things that are given for us and for our children, so that we may walk faithfully with the Lord and keep the covenant (Deut. 29:29). They have been revealed clearly. And because they have been revealed clearly they must be preached clearly.

And this is such a struggle for us. I think it has always been a struggle. Way back in the 4th Century the famous exegete Theodore of Mopsuestia had to point out the difference between the task of the commentator and the task of the preacher. The commentator, he said, has to work hard to tackle all the complexities and obscurities, all the details. But that's not

---

16.   Calvin, *Commentary on Deuteronomy* ad. loc.

The Priority of Preaching

the preacher's job. The preacher's job is 'to spread himself to his heart's content' on the great clear central truths of a passage.[17] It is always a temptation to do the commentator's job in the pulpit, so that we show off our learning but end up saying so much that we leave people confused. Dr Martyn Lloyd-Jones used to recount the anecdote of a woman listening to an enormously intellectual preacher. When asked if she enjoyed the sermon, she replied, 'Far be it from me to presume to understand such a great man as that!'[18]

William Griffiths was a fiery preacher on the Gower peninsular in South Wales in the early and mid-nineteenth century. He had a great passion for clear powerful preaching. He used to make notes on others' sermons. Of one he wrote, 'Not able to make anything of the sermon – persuaded that a hundred years of such preaching would produce no saving effects,'[19]

In the seventeenth century, John Owen, with all his famed learning, longed to preach in an accessible way. King Charles II used to find it mystifying that such a learned scholar should go to hear John Bunyan, an uneducated tinker, who spent much of his time in prison. When the King asked Owen about this, he replied, 'Could I possess the tinker's abilities for preaching, please your majesty, I would gladly relinquish all my learning.'[20] I too wish I had the tinker's power to be clear and to touch men's hearts.

The learned Calvin used to preach in Geneva in ordinary French so that any Genevan could understand it, without drawing attention to the great scholarship that lay behind his sermons.[21]

---

17. J.N.D. Kelly, *Golden Mouth: The Story of John Chrysostom* (Cornell University Press, 1995), p. 95

18. Martyn Lloyd-Jones. *Preaching and Preachers* (Zondervan, 1971), p. 122

19. *Pleasant Places: A Tribute to the Gower Ministry of Rev. B. Tudor Lloyd* (Gower Presbyterian Churches, 2006), p. 141

20. quoted in John Piper, *Tested by Fire: the fruit of affliction in the lives of John Bunyan, William Cowper, and David Brainerd* (IVP, 2001), p. 54

21. T.H.L. Parker, *Calvin's Preaching* (Edinburgh: T&T Clark, 1992), p. 86-89. The whole of chapter 9 is a clear and inspiring account of Calvin's expository method

J. C. Ryle was a highly educated man with a cultured and learned style. But when he ministered in rural parishes he realised they would not understand him; and so he 'crucified' his style.[22]

Luther, like so many whose ministries have been greatly used for the transformation of the church, was a distinguished scholar. But he was very insistent on the need for clarity and simplicity in his preaching: 'Cursed are all preachers that in the church aim at height and hard things, and, neglecting the saving health of the poor unlearned people, seek their own honour and praise, and therewith to please one or two ambitious persons. When I preach, I sink myself deep down. I regard neither Doctors nor Magistrates, of whom are here in this church above forty; but I have an eye to the multitude of young people, children, and servants, of whom are more than two thousand. I preach to those, directing myself to them that have need thereof. Will not the rest hear me? The door stands open unto them; they may begone.' He chides preachers who aim 'to please the worldly wise, and meantime neglect the simple and common multitude.' And he says that, 'to sprinkle out Hebrew, Greek, and Latin in their public sermons, savours merely of show...'[23]

Spurgeon says of some preachers that they 'think in smoke and preach in a cloud.'[24] But there is nothing spiritual about preaching in a fog of learning. We must strive for clarity, clarity, clarity. But not just clarity: we also need urgency, an urgent clarity, or a clear urgency.

(b) Urgency (clear urgency, or urgent clarity)
We must be clear, so that our hearers know what response of repentance and faith they must make. But we must also be

---

22. See his chapter 'Simplicity in preaching' in *The Upper Room* (Banner of Truth)

23. *The Table Talk of Martin Luther* trans. William Hazlitt, edited with an introduction by Thomas S. Kepler (Mineola, New York: Dover Publications, 2005) first published in German in 1566. Number 365, pp. 144-45. I am grateful to Lee Gatiss for this reference.

24. C.H. Spurgeon, *Lectures to my students* (London: Marshall, Morgan and Scott, 1954), p. 77f

urgent, for the response must be made today. A century ago P. T. Forsyth commented that people 'are very quick to *feel*, and keen to *know*; but they are not only slow, they are averse, to *decide*. Yet it is for decision that Christianity calls.'[25] Every scripture calls us today in some manner to repent and believe afresh, for the Christian just as much as for the non-Christian.

We must not think that only certain passages are possible or suitable for preaching Christ with urgency, whether to Christian or non-Christian. It is perfectly true that some contain the gospel more concisely and in a way that is easier to explain. Of course that is true. But in principle the whole Bible offers the whole Christ to all people. Some years ago I preached four sermons on the book of Haggai. Just recently a man told me he had taken a non-Christian friend to church on one of those Sundays, not realising the preacher was working through an obscure minor prophet hidden near the end of the Old Testament. When he saw the sermon passage his heart sank. But it was too late. His friend listened to Haggai. And his friend was converted! I confess to some astonishment on my own part when I heard that. It was not in any conventional sense an evangelistic sermon. But I trust that the urgency of faith was there; and by the grace of God that young man believed.

So let us preach with clear urgency. Let us not just teach, but also preach. If teaching is like the signpost which explains clearly to us where we ought to go and how to go there, preaching is like the friendly but firm shove from behind to get us started on actually going there and to keep us moving. We must teach: exhortation without teaching is like someone giving me a shove without explaining why. It is an act of verbal aggression, an invasion of my personal space, a ranting and raving without explaining to me why I need to do what the soap box warrior shouts at me that I must do. We must teach. If we do not teach with patience and clarity, there is

25. P.T. Forsyth, *Positive Preaching and the Modern Mind* (3rd Edition. London: Independent Press, 1949), p. 89

no point preaching. But we must not stop with teaching. It is a fine thing patiently to explain to me so that I understand. But if you love me you will press home to me with all the force you can my need to act on what I now understand, and to act on it today.

The story is told of three apprentice devils being trained by Satan. 'What are you going to try today?' asks the leader. The first apprentice replies, 'I'm going to tell them there is no God.' 'Well,' says Satan, 'you can try. A few fools will believe you. But the universe shouts the existence of God. There is evidence all around and you'll not do very well. Indeed, even in the secular twenty-first century you may find yourself witnessing the slow death of atheism. Any other ideas?' The second apprentice tries this: 'I'm going to tell them there's no judgment.' 'That's a better idea', says Satan. 'You will persuade more people of that, especially some of the clergy. But human beings have a gut sense of accountability, that actions have consequences. They know what it is to feel guilty even when their therapists tell them not to. So I think you'll find it an uphill struggle. Anyone else have an idea?' The third apprentice pipes up, 'I'm going to tell them there's no hurry.' 'Brilliant,' says Satan. 'That is just what you want to say. You will have great success. Let them listen to the word of God and whisper in their ears, "This is good stuff. One day you ought to do something about this. But tomorrow will do."'

We must preach with clear urgency and urgent clarity. And to do so we will need hearts filled with a passionate longing for our preaching to be heeded.

(c) Passion

Moses preaches as a dying man. He knows he cannot go into the land. And so he preaches with passion. He cares deeply about his message, his God and his hearers. The story is told of a young girl listening to the famous evangelical Charles Simeon preaching fervently in Holy Trinity, Cambridge, in the 1780's.

The child is said to have looked up at her mother and asked, 'O mama, what is the gentleman in a passion about?'[26] Like Moses, the gentleman was in a passion about the God who is a consuming fire, the stubborn human heart, and the urgency of faith.

We must not preach with what Spurgeon called, 'articulate snoring.'[27] I can remember once going to sleep on my feet while teaching in a school. Happily I was teaching maths, so it didn't matter. It was a warm summer's afternoon and I guess I was only unconscious for a second or two. I continued talking on autopilot and I hope the pupils didn't notice. But I had definitely dropped off and had consciously to think where I was! We must not do this in the pulpit.

Richard Baxter said that, 'a sleepy preacher will hardly awaken drowsy sinners ... Speak to people as to men that must be awakened ...' He expressed his earnestness in his poem 'Love Breathing Thanks and Praise' in which he wrote of his ministry as follows.

> 'Still thinking I had little time to live,
> My fervent heart to win men's souls did strive.
> I preached as never sure to preach again,
> And as a dying man to dying men!
> O how should preachers men's repenting crave
> Who see how near the Church is to the grave?
> And see that while we preach and hear, we die,
> Rapt by swift time to vast eternity!' [28]

This is not a matter of style. Some of our African brethren have said to me at Cornhill that their more energetic preaching style doesn't necessarily mean anything in terms of spiritual substance. No, they say, it is perfectly possible to preach with

26. Hugh Evan Hopkins, *Charles Simeon of Cambridge* (Hodder and Stoughton, 1977), p. 65
27. quoted in John R.W. Stott *I Believe in Preaching* (IVP, 1982), p. 275
28. Richard Baxter, *Poetical Fragments* (1681; Gregg International Publishers, 1971), p. 39f, quoted in John R.W. Stott, *I believe in Preaching* (Hodder and Stoughton, 1962), p. 277

tremendous physical and emotional energy and just to be doing the culturally normal thing and going through the motions. In fact some of them are deliberately playing down the emotional style to avoid precisely that danger. We must not mistake an emotional style for a heart of passion.

Conversely, it is possible to preach in a very reserved manner but to have fire burning in every bone of the preacher's body. It is said of the great American preacher Jonathan Edwards that he 'preached in a virtual monotone, a cushion under his elbow as he propped his head above the dense script, which he read word for word.'[29] They said of him that he preached as though he were staring at the bell-rope at the back of the meeting-house![30] So we must not equate passion with style.

But we must have hearts aflame with passion. Dr. Martyn Lloyd-Jones famously defined preaching as, 'Logic on fire! Eloquent reason! ... Preaching is theology coming through a man who is on fire.'[31] The story is told that when W. E. Sangster was interviewing a candidate for the ministry, the nervous young man explained that he was quite shy and not the sort of person ever to set the River Thames on fire. 'My dear young brother,' responded Sangster, 'I'm not interested to know if you could set the Thames on fire. What I want to know is this: if I picked you up by the scruff of your neck and dropped you into the Thames, would it sizzle?'[32] Never mind his eloquence; was he himself on fire?

This is about the heart. As J. I. Packer used to say to aspiring preachers, 'Read yourself full, think yourself clear, pray yourself hot, let yourself go.' There is little worse than listening to a theologically correct sermon which is taught as a lecture, where we wonder if the text has got anywhere near the preacher's heart, where the exercise seems to be from head

---

29. William J.U. Philip, *Concerning Preaching* (PT Media Paper, no. 1, 2002), p. 20
30. George M. Marsden, *Jonathan Edwards: A Life* (Yale University Press, 2003), p. 220
31. D. Martyn Lloyd-Jones, *Preaching and Preachers* (Hodder and Stoughton, 1971), p. 97
32. John R.W. Stott, *I believe in Preaching* (Hodder and Stoughton, 1962), p. 285

to head, from intellect to intellect (or worse still, from the preacher's notes to the hearer's notes without passing through the mind of either). Someone said to a friend of mine that we ought to be able to hear from the preacher's tone of voice the most important point of the sermon.

A century ago P. T. Forsyth warned against thinking that our preaching is merely educative rather than evangelical, that we might slip into thinking that preaching is 'something *said* with more or less force, instead of something *done* with more or less power.'[33]

I had an instructive experience when preaching for a winter Sunday evening meeting in the church to which I now belong. I was five minutes or so into a half-hour sermon when the lights went out because of an electrical fault and we were plunged into deep darkness. Now I was brought up in a strange English culture in which it is polite to ignore anything that goes wrong and carry on as if everything is fine. So instinctively I just kept going. After all, I still had my voice and my hearers still had their ears. It was true that I couldn't see my notes for a few minutes (until a helpful friend found a torch). But that was the point: What happened tested the extent to which the passage I was preaching was laid clearly and passionately on my heart. As it happens, that week it was, and so although I dare say the preaching became a bit more ragged, a bit less tidy, nevertheless I was able to continue with reasonable coherence, and with genuine passionate engagement with my hearers.

Reflecting on this experience gave me an idea. It seems to me that any preacher ought to be able to continue his sermon without his notes if necessary. We would not expect him to be as tidy or precise; but we would expect him to be able in some manner to expound the heart of the text as it has been laid on his own heart through his careful preparation and understanding with his mind. Here's the idea: In the Cornhill Training Course one of the core ingredients is practice classes

---

33. P.T. Forsyth, *Positive Preaching and the Modern Mind* (3rd Edition. London: Independent Press, 1949), p. 35

where students give sermons or Bible teaching talks. Suppose we agreed that at some stage in a practice sermon the group leader could quietly ask for our notes, and then expect us to continue without them. It would be a bit like the driving test where the examiner calls out for an emergency stop. We know he or she is going to make this call at some stage; we just don't know when. I suppose it would be rather alarming for students, and it might discourage applicants! But it would be a healthy exercise. We ought to have the central message of our passage so clearly and warmly engraved on our hearts that we could speak it, at least approximately, without our notes.

Let us strive for urgent clear passion, clear passionate urgency and passionate urgent clarity.

THEME 4. THE WONDER OF GRACE

My final theme in this chapter is the most important. Moses never forgets the wonder of grace as he offers Christ to the people. I love that refrain in John Wesley's diaries, 'I offered Christ to the people.' '(Moses) wrote about me,' said Jesus (John 5:46). Moses was, in anticipation and foreshadowing, a preacher of grace and therefore a preacher of Christ.

In Deuteronomy 30:11-14 Moses repeatedly tells the Israelites not only that they can understand the covenant, but that they can actually do it. It is possible for this word so to dwell in their heart and therefore to come out of their mouth (and not just go in their ears) that they will be able to do it (v. 14). That is to say, they can be faithful to the covenant God. We ask, how is this possible? Surely the whole point of the law is that the people were unable to do it. After all, when Joshua challenged the people to be faithful to the LORD, and they replied rather shallowly and tritely, 'Far be it from us to forsake the LORD to serve other gods!' (You don't think *we'd* do anything terrible like that, do you?) Joshua replied, 'You are *not* able to serve the LORD. He is a holy God; he is a jealous God. He will not forgive your rebellion and your sins' (Josh. 24:16-20). So what can Moses mean?

Given that Jesus says Moses spoke of him, it seems that Moses was, in principle, offering them Christ. That is to say, he was calling them to believe the God of promise. And whenever an Old Testament saint believed the promises, in principle he believed in the Christ in whom all those promises would be fulfilled and guaranteed (2 Cor. 1:20, 'For no matter how many promises God has made, they are "Yes" in Christ.')

That Moses was preaching grace is confirmed in Deut. 30:15-20 (ESV). He sets before them 'life and prosperity, death and destruction'. But he does not then challenge them, 'Therefore try harder, do your best to keep the law and to be loyal to God.' Instead he says, 'Therefore choose life'. The choice Moses sets before them is not the choice between bad works and good works, or between half-hearted works and whole-hearted works; it is the choice between works and grace. 'Therefore choose life', means, therefore, choose grace, trust the God of promise (v. 20).

In some ways the choice Moses offers them is obvious. I remember hearing a somewhat irreverent sketch by the comedian Eddie Izzard about the Church of England. He imagines an absurd church tea-party where guests are asked 'would you like cake or death?' They tend to choose cake! Moses' choice is a bit like that: would you like blessing, long life in the land, prosperity, or would you like a nasty, brutish and short life in the land followed by exile and death? It really ought to be a no-brainer.

And yet Moses knows they will choose death, because he knows the human heart. And he knows that only God can change it. And yet Moses still believes in grace.[34] Again and again Moses speaks of the promise to Abraham, Isaac and Jacob (e.g. Deut. 30:20). He believes God will fulfil this promise – and not only the promise of the land, but the promise to which the land points, which is the new heavens and new earth.

---

34. Paul A. Barker, *The Triumph of Grace in Deuteronomy* (Paternoster, 2004)

The great paradox of Deuteronomy is that the story goes on when it ought to end. It ought to end in tears and the curtain come down to end the drama, time after time. It ought to end in the desert, and yet God was determined 'to do you good in the end' (Deut. 8:16 ESV). It ought to end at the golden calf. It ought to end at Baal-Peor. It ought to end at the exile. And yet the story goes on. So although there are tears along the way, it will not end in tears.

How is this so? Because the God who made the promise will keep the promise. And yet how can he keep the promise, since the promise is so clearly conditional? *If* you are faithful and loyal, you will live long in the land, but *if* you are not, you won't. So how can the promise be at the same time conditional and certain? In the Old Testament this is the great paradox of faith: how is he going to do it? The answer must be that he himself will somehow fulfil the conditions of the covenant so that he can make certain the promise of the covenant.

I take it that Moses only saw this hazily; the prophets after him also searched and enquired as the Spirit of Christ within them spoke of the sufferings and the subsequent glory (1 Pet. 1:10-11). One day a man would obey the covenant, and by his obedience would make many righteous (Rom. 5:19), and by his sin-bearing, curse-bearing work would make it possible for hearts to be circumcised (to fulfil the promise of Deut. 30:6). But in the meantime, Moses preaches Christ in foreshadowing and promise. And those who believed the God of promise believed in principle in Christ. This is why he says that they can do the word he preaches (Deut. 30:11-14). Paul expounds precisely this passage (Deut. 30:11-14) in Romans 10:6-9, in the context of faith in Christ. Paul makes it clear that in the word Moses preached, Christ was offered to the people.[35]

---

35. see Christopher Ash, *Teaching Romans* (PT Media/Christian Focus, 2009) on Romans 10:6-9

Application: confident grace

We too are to offer Christ in our preaching and to do so with confidence. It would be easy to hear all this emphasis on urgency and passion and to think we must panic. I love the story told by a senior White House staffer who served under President Richard Nixon when Henry Kissinger was Secretary of State. This staffer recounted how the senior staff gathered in the Oval Office early each morning. I expect he exaggerated, but he recounted how on almost every day Kissinger said, 'Mr. President, the decision we are going to take today will affect the entire course of human history.' After a couple of years of that, he said, you get tired! Or, as Paul puts it, 'Who is sufficient for these things?' (2 Cor. 2:16 ESV).

So I want to end this chapter like this. There is an irony in taking Moses' preaching under the title, 'Preaching that transforms the church'. Because, for all Moses' engagement, for all his clarity, for all his urgency, for all his passion, for all his offering of Christ to the people, by and large they were unchanged. They might as well have been David Copperfield looking out of the window as Moses preached. The same was true of Isaiah's preaching (Isa. 53:1, 'Who has believed our message and to whom has the arm of the LORD been revealed?' Not many). The same was true of the LORD Jesus' preaching (e.g. John 6:66f. 'From this time many of his disciples turned back and no longer followed him').

But urgent preaching is not frenetic preaching, or panicky preaching. Rather it is rooted in a quiet confidence that the God who made the promises will fulfil them in his time and his way, that his word will not return to him empty but will accomplish what he desires (Isa. 55:10-11). So we may preach passionately and yet with a calm assurance in his sovereign grace. Bishop John Jewel put it like this in the 1560's, 'Let us persevere with our task and leave the success to the LORD … for, as it is our duty to instruct the people with words, so it belongs to God to join to His words faith and force.'[36]

---

36. quoted in Peter Adam, *Speaking God's Words* (IVP, 1996), p. 119f

Conscious of the wonder of this word of Christ, we must pray. It is said of Spurgeon that as he slowly mounted the fifteen curving steps up to the pulpit in the Metropolitan Tabernacle, he muttered to himself on each step, 'I believe in the Holy Ghost'. Whether that is true or not (and I hope it is), Spurgeon certainly believed in the necessity of the work of the Spirit. For he wrote, 'The gospel is preached in the ears of all; it only comes with power to some. The power that is in the gospel does not lie in the eloquence of the preacher; otherwise men would be converters of souls. Nor does it lie in the preacher's learning; otherwise it would consist in the wisdom of men. We might preach till our tongues rotted, till we should exhaust our lungs and die, but never a soul would be converted unless there were mysterious power going with it – the Holy Ghost changing the will of man. O Sirs! We might as well preach to stone walls as preach to humanity unless the Holy Ghost be with the word, to give it power to convert the soul.'[37]

Like Moses, let us set before our hearers 'life and prosperity, death and destruction', conscious of the God who is consuming fire, deeply engaged with human hearts and human culture, impressing on ourselves and on our hearers the urgency of faith, but above all let us be confident in the wonder of grace as we offer Christ to the people. May God help us to do that.

---

37.   quoted in John R.W. Stott, *I believe in Preaching* ((Hodder and Stoughton, 1982) p. 334f.

3

Preaching that Mends a Broken World

Deuteronomy 4:5-14 (NIV)

[5]See, I have taught you decrees and laws as the LORD my God commanded me, so that you may follow them in the land you are entering to take possession of it. [6]Observe them carefully, for this will show your wisdom and understanding to the nations, who will hear about all these decrees and say, "Surely this great nation is a wise and understanding people." [7]What other nation is so great as to have their gods near them the way the LORD our God is near us whenever we pray to him? [8]And what other nation is so great as to have such righteous decrees and laws as this body of laws I am setting before you today?

[9]Only be careful, and watch yourselves closely so that you do not forget the things your eyes have seen or let them slip from your heart as long as you live. Teach them to your children and to their children after them. [10]Remember the day you stood before the LORD your God at Horeb, when he said to me, "Assemble the people before me to hear my words so that they may learn to revere me as long as they live in the land and may teach them to their children." [11]You came near and stood at the foot of the mountain while it blazed with fire to the very heavens, with black clouds and deep darkness.

[12]Then the LORD spoke to you out of the fire. You heard the sound of words but saw no form; there was only a voice. [13]He declared to you his covenant, the Ten Commandments, which he commanded you to follow and then wrote them on two stone tablets. [14]And the LORD directed me at that time to teach you the decrees and laws you are to follow in the land that you are crossing the Jordan to possess.

REBUILDING A BROKEN WORLD

My text for this third chapter is three words from Deuteronomy 4:10, 'Assemble the people...' My theme is preaching that mends a broken world, and my main focus is on the assembly of the people of God under the preached word of God.

How is a broken world to be reassembled? My family gave me a wonderful spherical jigsaw of the world. It had 500 rigid pieces that fitted together to make a perfect globe. We started (that is, I with my daughter Lizzie and my daughter-in-law Katie) with 500 pieces scattered on the floor, a picture of a fractured world. It was a great feeling to put the North Pole in place, and to feel that we had assembled a fractured globe. But that feeling is as nothing when compared with the feeling God will have at the end of time, when he finally reassembles a broken world under one head, the LORD Jesus Christ (Eph. 1:10).

Many Christians, and especially pastor-teachers, carry around with us something of the pain of a broken world, perhaps in marriages and families, or in local neighbourhoods. I was walking home ten days before I gave the address on which this chapter is based, and I had to detour because within the previous hour a fourteen-year-old boy had been stabbed on my route home, and police were cordoning off the area. He died some weeks later, and five months later flowers are still being laid by the pavement where he was attacked. We feel the pain of this broken world, of violence, of misery, of hatred, and sometimes it breaks in close to home. There is an Arab proverb: 'I against my brother, my brother and I against my cousin, my cousin and I against the world.' Sometimes it feels like that. We hold broken marriages, broken families, broken people, in our hearts.

Sometimes we must wonder whether the way we spend our week is really the best way to help. I did, when that teenager was stabbed. I wanted to do something to help, perhaps by giving my energies to some local project to help children at risk or those liable to be drawn into the culture of the gangs and knife crime. Is it really helping when we spend so much of our week labouring at the word of God, preparing to preach it to the churches we serve? Isn't this really an irrelevance, a waste of time? Is it worth slogging away preparing Sunday's sermon with such a world of need outside? Are we not, as one sceptic put it, 'Fiddling in Bible land, while Rome burns'? Isn't what we're about as preachers simply irrelevant to a broken world?

It certainly is a broken world. A few years ago it was popular to hail 'multiculturalism' as a strategy that would bring harmony to Britain, a way to hold together such a wide variety of peoples. And yet one of its former advocates, Jonathan Sacks, the Chief Rabbi, now writes: 'Multiculturalism has run its course, and it is time to move on. It was a fine, even noble idea in its time. It was designed to make ethnic and religious minorities feel more at home in society ... It affirmed their culture. It gave dignity to difference', and yet it hasn't worked: 'It has led not to integration but to segregation... It was intended to promote tolerance. Instead, the result has been ... societies more abrasive, fractured and intolerant than they once were.'[1]

So it didn't work. What are we to do about it? Let me put my thesis on the table. When you or I stand to preach in a local church, we see before us the seeds of reassembly for a broken world. And we have in our mouths the DNA of those seeds. As we preach to them week by week, those seeds grow and are shaped by grace. And we and they together form the societies

1. Jonathan Sacks, *The Home We Build Together: Recreating Society* (Continuum, 2007) p. 3

that alone can rebuild a broken world by grace. As Peter puts it (1 Pet.1:22-25), new birth comes by an imperishable seed, and that seed is the preached word ('...you have been born again, not of perishable seed, but of imperishable, through the living and enduring word of God.... And this is the word that was preached to you'). And that seed will rebuild the world. When every other strategy is seen to fail, the preaching of the word of Christ will be seen for what it is, God's strategy to reassemble a broken world. That's my thesis.

Preachers don't often feel like that. We may be much more conscious of who is not there on Sunday, or of the sheer depressing dysfunctionality of church life, of the weakness and smallness of it all. But I want to lift our minds and hearts to see what is happening when we preach, and the place our preaching has in God's strategy to mend a broken world under Christ.

Our subject continues to be the priority of preaching. My aim is to encourage us to persevere with this demanding work, not to get side-tracked by subsidiary priorities, not to give up, not to listen to the voice on our shoulder that tells us it's not worthwhile. Our focus in chapter one was authority. We took those words, 'listen to him', listen to the word of the living God in the mouth of the preacher of Christ. The expository preacher has a real authority; but it is a borrowed authority, borrowed only with great toil, humility and pain. We distinguished preaching from discussion, Bible reading, and even Bible study in a group. We saw how the preached word expresses most clearly the authority of Christ in the written word. We considered how, while the written word is the logical locus of God's authority, the preached word is the practical expression of that authority, in which God speaks to us by the voice of a man.

Then in chapter 2 we took the theme of urgency, passion and engagement. We considered the distinction, that preaching is more than just teaching, and how preaching is to be a spiritual event in which Christ is offered to men and women by the preached word, and urged on men and women by urgent appeal, by a preacher who is engaged with people and culture and speaks not in a moronic monologue but rather is engaged in a silent dialogue speaking to people he knows, loves and understands.

In this chapter I want to turn the focus around and look not so much at the preacher as at the congregation, the assembly, and to think together about how preaching and assembly are related. We consider the local church assembly. First I want us to see it signalled in Deuteronomy. Then I want to pull back and see it on its wider Bible canvas. Finally I want to suggest four practical areas of application for preaching today.

A. The Assembly in Deuteronomy: the standard shape of the church is the Assembly called together by, and under, the word of God

Deuteronomy signals in four ways the standard shape of the church:

1. *Sinai (or Horeb) is the pattern for the assembly*

We'll begin in Deuteronomy 4:10. Moses says to Israel, 'Remember the day you stood before the Lord your God at Horeb, when he said to me, "Assemble the people before me to hear my words so that they may learn to revere me as long as they live in the land and may teach them to their children."'

At Horeb the people were assembled or gathered at the command of God (God gave the command, '*Assemble* the people before me …'). And they were assembled to hear that word ('Assemble the people … *to hear my words*'). They were called together by the word of God and they were called together to listen to the word of God.

Three times in Deuteronomy Moses refers back to that great formative day simply as 'the day of the assembly' (the Hebrew word *qahal*) (Deut. 9:10; 10:4; 18:16). In each case the context refers to the word of God given at that assembly.

(a) Deuteronomy 9:10, 'The Lord gave me two stone tablets inscribed by the finger of God. On them were all the commandments the Lord proclaimed to you on the mountain out of the fire, *on the day of the assembly.*'

(b) Deuteronomy 10:4, 'The LORD wrote on these tablets what he had written before, the Ten Commandments (lit. 'ten words') he had proclaimed to you on the mountain, out of the fire, *on the day of the assembly*.'

(c) Finally, and very significantly, in 18:15-16, in the passage we considered in chapter one about the prophet like Moses, Moses says, 'The LORD your God will raise up for you a prophet like me from among your own brothers. You must listen to him. For this is what you asked of the LORD your God at Horeb *on the day of the assembly* when you said, "Let us not hear the voice of the LORD our God nor see this great fire any more, or we will die."'

The day of that assembly became the prototype for every assembly of the people of God. That is where preaching happens. So, for example, Qoheleth (the preacher in Ecclesiastes) is the one who speaks in the *qahal*. Preaching and assembly are inseparable. Preaching, properly understood, cannot be done by telecommunication, but only in assembly. We will come back to this point.

So the fundamental and normative pattern for this supernatural assembly is that it is gathered by the word of God and under the spoken word of God. We are to listen to God by listening to his prophets, not on our own, but in assembly.

2.   Israel is defined by the assembly and therefore by the word in the assembly
Israel is the *qahal* or the *ecclesia*, the church in the wilderness, as Stephen calls it in Acts 7:38. An Israelite belongs to the assembly even when they are not assembled. We see this, for example, when the assembly is summoned by the trumpeters in Numbers 10:7 and 20:10. The assembly exists even when it is not assembled. The trumpeters do not create the assembly; they summon the assembly that already exists, so that the assembly comes together. Israel is not a collection of individuals who sometimes assemble; it is an assembly whose members may sometimes be dispersed.

This is not an assembly of any random people who feel like gathering. It is an assembly whose boundaries are defined and guarded. In Deuteronomy 23:2-8 there are laws regulating who may or may not be admitted into the assembly of Israel in generations to come. Again and again in Deuteronomy when the boundaries of the assembly are to be guarded by discipline, Moses says, 'You must purge the evil from among you' (13:5; 17:7, 12; 19:19; 22:21f., 24; 24:7). The worst thing about those terrible judgments (including capital punishment) was that they placed someone outside the assembly of Israel for ever.

So we have here an assembly, properly constituted with an institutional dimension, with boundaries. This is not a gathering of those who happen to decide to gather on that particular day.

3. The assembly of Israel is at the 'place' God chooses

After Moses has written the law, in Deuteronomy 31, he gives it to the priests and the elders of Israel with the following instructions: 'At the end of every seven years, in the year for cancelling debts, during the Feast of Tabernacles, when all Israel comes to appear before the LORD your God *at the place he will choose*, you shall read this law before them in their hearing. *Assemble the people* – men, women and children, and the aliens living in your towns – so that they can listen and learn to fear the LORD your God and follow carefully all the words of this law' (Deut. 31:10-12).

The assembly ('Assemble the people…') is in 'the place he will choose'. This 'place' is very important in Deuteronomy. The main block of laws from chapters 12–26 is bracketed by two very significant chapters about 'the place the LORD your God will choose …to put his Name there for his dwelling' (Deut. 12:5).

Chapter 12 introduces that place and tells them to go to that one place (Deut. 12:5, 14, 18, 21, 26) and not to lots of different places (12:2, 'all the places on the high mountains and on the hills and under every spreading tree where the nations you are dispossessing worship their gods'; Deut. 12:13, 'anywhere you please', NRSV 'any place you happen to see'; cf. Jer. 3:6).

And then chapter 26 rounds off the laws by the ceremony of the first-fruits which are again brought to 'the place that

中

the LORD your God will choose as a dwelling for his Name' (Deut. 26:2). In between chapters 12 and 26 'the place' keeps cropping up in the laws (e.g. Deut. 14:23-25; 15:20; 16:2, 6, 7, 11, 15, 16; 17:8, 10 etc.)

'The place' was not always Jerusalem, as was wrongly assumed by de Wette in 1805, with his theory that the whole thing was a later invention to justify King Josiah's centralising reforms (2 Kings 22f.), the theory later popularised by Wellhausen.[2] 'The place' seems to have been a different place at different times. It was Shiloh at one stage (Jer. 7:12 'the place in Shiloh where I first made a dwelling for my Name'), and certainly it was Zion at the end.

But the key point about 'the place' is that it is singular. Because the LORD is *one* (Deut. 6:4), his people must be one and gather to one place. That is where his worship will be shaped by his word. There is a close connection between the place and the law, so much so that when the word of God is neglected in the place, as it was in the Temple of Jeremiah's day, God brings the word to the entrance of the place by an outsider, as we see in Jeremiah's famous Temple sermon (Jer. 7).

4.   The assembly is to be of 'all Israel'

Lastly, we note that the assembly was to be of 'all Israel': 'At the end of every seven years, …when *all Israel* comes to appear before the LORD your God at the place he will choose, you shall read this law …' (Deut. 31:10-11). Right at the start (Deut. 1:1), we read that, 'These are the words Moses spoke to all Israel …' This is repeated in Deuteronomy 5:1 and Deuteronomy 31:1, and echoed in the address, 'Hear, O Israel' (Deut. 4:1; 6:4; 9:1, and cf. 20:2ff., where the same address is to be made by the priest in the future). These preached words are to be heard by the whole people of God assembled in one place. It was not just once that 'all Israel' was called to gather; this is the instruction for the regular seven-yearly gathering (Deut. 31:11).

2.   J.G. McConville, *Deuteronomy* (IVP Apollos, 2002), p. 21f. convincingly argues against de Wette's theory

This motif of 'all Israel' is picked up particularly by the Chronicler. So for example in 1 Chronicles 13:5 when the Ark is to be brought up to Jerusalem, 'David assembled all the Israelites (ESV 'all Israel')…' (or 1 Chron. 28:8 '…all Israel…the assembly of the LORD').

The significance of 'all Israel' is that we have one people gathered in the one place, the whole people, not any subsection of the people. It may be 'all Israel' in the persons of their senior representatives, or it may be the whole assembly literally. But the point is that it cannot just be a homogeneous subset of Israel, such as 'all the wood-cutters of Israel' or 'all the middle-aged fathers of Israel'.

So Deuteronomy foreshadows for us as the normative shape of the church an assembly called together by the word of God, called together to hear the preached word of God, called together as a place of unity of the whole people of God, and called together under grace and so filled with joy. This is the day of the assembly. In these four ways Deuteronomy makes it clear that the preaching of the word of God is inseparable from the assembly of the people of God.

B. THE ASSEMBLY ON ITS WIDER BIBLICAL CANVAS

Let's now take a step back and look at the assembly on its wider Bible canvas. The motif of scattering and gathering makes a fascinating and illuminating way into the whole Bible story of judgment and salvation. A Bible overview could be constructed around this organising theme. We shall note five features of scattering and gathering, and take them in the order 1, 2, 3, 5 and finally 4, for a reason that will become clear.

1. *False worship always leads to scattering*

In Deuteronomy 4:25-28 Moses warns the people that if, after they have lived in the land for a time, 'you then become corrupt and make any kind of idol, doing evil in the eyes of the LORD your God and provoking him to anger, I call heaven and earth as witnesses against you this day that you will quickly perish from the land that you are crossing the Jordan to possess. You will not live there long but will certainly be destroyed. The LORD will scatter you among the peoples, and only a few of you will survive among the nations to which the LORD will drive you.'

Moses warns them that if they don't gather, assembled by and under the word of God; if instead they choose their own worship, shape their own idols, what happens? Answer: verse 27, 'The LORD will scatter you'. False worship is why we live in a broken world. We see this again in Deuteronomy 28:64 in the covenant curses ('Then the LORD will scatter you among all nations, from one end of the earth to the other.')

From Babel onwards (Gen. 11:1-9) human pride has brought upon itself the judgement of divine scattering. I build my tower with me at the centre and you build your tower with yourself at the centre and so there is bound to be war. In the absence of the unifying voice of God, all we are left with is the divisive babble (Babel) of our own voices.

2. *God promises to gather a reassembled world*

But the promise to Abraham – Genesis 12, so soon after Babel in Genesis 11 – carried with it the promise of remaking a broken world. When Isaac retells this promise in his blessing of Jacob in Genesis 28:3 he says, 'May God Almighty bless you and make you fruitful and increase your numbers until you become a community (lit. an assembly, a gathering, a *qahal*) of peoples.' This same word *qahal*, assembly, is repeated in Gen. 35:11 when God promises Jacob, 'I am God Almighty; be fruitful and increase in number. A nation and a community (assembly, *qahal*) of nations will come from you...' Jacob repeats this to Joseph's sons in Genesis 48:3-4, 'God Almighty appeared to me at Luz in the land of Canaan, and there he blessed me and said to me, "I am going to make you fruitful and will increase your numbers. I will make you a community (assembly, *qahal*) of peoples..."'

This is what God does in salvation: he gathers, he assembles, he reassembles a broken world. God has never been in the business of saving individuals as individuals, but always of reassembling a fractured world. And he does it by his preached word of grace. Humankind is scattered by sin and gathered by grace.

We see this gathering in the assembly of Nehemiah 8 at the end of the exile, where 'all Israel' gathered 'as one man' (Neh. 8:1) in the market-place of Jerusalem, scattered by the judgment of exile, but now gathered under the word of grace as Ezra preaches to them.

We see this vividly in the great vision of Isaiah 2:1-5 (or Micah 4:1-5), where all the nations of the world, with all their swords and spears, their war and strife, go up to Jerusalem, because it is the place where God teaches his ways, and out of which goes his gracious instruction. And under his word their swords are beaten into ploughshares, their spears into pruning hooks. God is in the business of gathering a scattered world. And he does it by his word. When we listen to our own babble, we are scattered. When we assemble under his word, we are gathered.

3. *That promise of gathering begins to be fulfilled when the place of assembly moves – in Biblical imagery – from Sinai to Zion. That is to say, it begins to be fulfilled in Jesus Christ.*

The day of the assembly at Sinai or Horeb was a paradoxical day. For it was a day when they were called to assemble but forbidden to draw near. They gathered to the mountain, but they dared not touch. If even a beast touched the mountain, it had to be killed by stoning so that its executioners were not brought into contact with anything that had been in contact with the mountain (Exod. 19:12, 13). It was a meeting with God, but a meeting at arm's length (to put it mildly), a meeting that made even Moses tremble with fear.

And the writer to the Hebrews (Heb. 12:18-29) is filled with awe and wonder as he teaches Christian people about our assemblies. I take it that when the writer says, 'You have not come… You have come…' (vv. 18, 22), he speaks of the heavenly assembly as it is expressed concretely in our local church assemblies. He is interested in the actual assembling together of God's people (cf. Heb. 10:25, 'Let us not give up meeting together...'). He is filled with awe because we have not come to Sinai. Thank God, we have not come to that place of terror, distance and forbidden access.

And yet there are at least four ways in which our assemblies are like that paradigmatic assembly at Sinai. First (and most obviously), we still assemble. Secondly, we still assemble in the presence of God. At Zion, as at Sinai, we have come 'to God, the judge of all' (Heb. 12:23). Thirdly, the God in whose presence we assemble is still 'a consuming fire' (Heb. 12:29), just as he always was and always will be. Fourthly, we still assemble to hear and heed his word (Heb. 12:25, 'See to it that you do not refuse him who speaks.')

So our assembly in the local church is still patterned on 'the day of the Assembly' at Horeb in these four ways: it is still an assembly, still an assembly in the presence of God, still an assembly in the presence of God who is a consuming fire, and still an assembly to hear and heed his word.

But the place has moved (in Biblical imagery) from Sinai to Zion, to the place where the blood of the covenant has been shed, to the place where the mediator of a better covenant welcomes us, takes us by the hand and brings us to God (1 Pet. 3:18). This is now the place where we draw near with confidence. It is no longer a gathering for distance, but an assembly for access. All this was foreshadowed even at Sinai, by the blood of the covenant sprinkled on the people (Exod. 24:6-8), and by the blood of the Passover lamb saving the firstborn. When the writer to the Hebrews calls the assembly 'the assembly of the firstborn' (Heb. 12:23) he seems to mean those covered by the Passover blood (Heb. 11:28), sprinkled by faith so that the destroyer of the firstborn might not touch them.

Interestingly, there is an anticipation of this new covenant assembly even in the old covenant assemblies of Israel, not at

Sinai, but in the great assemblies of Israel after that. Because –
perhaps surprisingly – those later old covenant assemblies were
to be places of joy, and therefore presumably places of grace.
This may come as something of a surprise, given the terror
of Mt. Sinai. But the assemblies of Israel, patterned on Sinai,
were to be places not of terror but of joy, even under the old
covenant.

When it is first introduced in Deuteronomy 12 the 'place'
is a place for rejoicing in the presence of God: 'There, in the
presence of the LORD your God, you and your families shall
eat and shall *rejoice* in everything you have put your hand to …
And there *rejoice* before the LORD your God, you, your sons and
daughters, your menservants and maidservants, and the Levites
from your towns, who have no allotment or inheritance of their
own … and you are to *rejoice* before the LORD your God …'
(Deut. 12:7, 12, 18).

In Deuteronomy 16 the great festivals of Passover, Weeks,
and Booths (Tabernacles) are taught. Notice for example in
Deuteronomy 16:11-12 for the Feast of Weeks, 'And *rejoice* before
the LORD your God at the place he will choose as a dwelling for
his Name – you, your sons and daughters, your menservants
and maidservants, the Levites in your towns, and the aliens, the
fatherless and the widows living among you. Remember that
you were slaves in Egypt…' There is the joy of redemption in
these gatherings. The place is a place of inclusive rejoicing at
the overflowing grace and goodness of God.

Notice again in Deuteronomy 16:14-15, for Tabernacles, '*Be
joyful* at your Feast – you, your sons and daughters, your menservants and maidservants, and the Levites, the aliens, the fatherless and the widows who live in your towns. For seven days cel-
ebrate the Feast to the LORD your God at the place the LORD will
choose. For the LORD your God will bless you in all your harvest
and in all the work of your hands, and *your joy will be complete.*'

So there is a trajectory, in Biblical imagery, from the scattering
of Babel, via the promise of gathering given to the patriarchs,

to the day of the assembly at Horeb, and then to Zion, to the place of the blood of the mediator. In Biblical language, Jesus is 'the place' where 'all Israel' assembles in the gathering of the local church.

5.   *The trajectory ends around the throne in the new creation*

In the LORD Jesus Christ a broken world will be reassembled. He is the one who gathers, and he who does not gather with him, assemble with him, scatters (Matt. 12:30). John comments that when Caiaphas said it was better for Israel that Jesus should die for the people than that the whole nation should perish, he spoke more truly than he knew. In particular, Caiaphas 'prophesied that Jesus would die for the Jewish nation, and not only for that nation but also for the *scattered* children of God, to *bring them together and make them one*' (John 11:51-52). Jesus is in the assembly business. And it is the grand purpose of God 'when the times will have reached their fulfilment – to bring all things in heaven and on earth together under one head, even Christ' (Eph. 1:10).

That reassembly began to be visible dramatically at Pentecost, when the Babel (babble) scattering of languages was vividly reversed as a signpost to what God was beginning to do in Jesus all over the world. One day that reassembly will be complete, and there will be 'a great multitude that no-one could count, from every nation, tribe, people and language, standing before the throne and in front of the Lamb' (Rev. 7:9). One day God will do through the church what multiculturalism has failed to do, what every human strategy will fail to do. He will rebuild a broken world.

4.   *In the meantime we have the local church, who are 'dispersed assemblies'*

But there's a gap. Babel – Promise – Sinai – Zion – ………. – the Throne. Before we reach the throne, in the meantime, we have the local church. Paul seems happy to draw a pretty straight line from 'the day of the assembly' in the wilderness to the life of the local church. In 1 Corinthians 5, in the context of local church discipline, he caps his argument quite simply by echoing the Deuteronomy refrain, 'Expel the wicked man from among you' (1 Cor. 5:13). The assembly of the local Christian church is patterned on the day of the assembly at Sinai, now gloriously transformed by Jesus into an assembly for access.

But the problem is that we no longer have even the pretence of 'all Israel' in one place; we have local churches in many places. So what has happened to the theme of gathering? We seem to have scattering to the ends of the earth! On the face of it, my suggestion that the Bible story may be told in terms of scattering for judgment and gathering for grace has gone up in flames with the Great Commission. We were scattered by sin; we expect to be gathered by grace; but instead we find ourselves scattered to the ends of the earth by the Great Commission to go into all the world.

But it's not as simple as that. In local churches we no longer have a scattering of individuals under judgment (for this would be the punishment of exile); instead we have scattered gatherings, dispersed assemblies, if that is not an oxymoron, a contradiction in terms. All over the world, the local church is a counter-cultural sign in a fragmented world that reassembly is taking place, but is not finished yet. The local church shows this in two ways. Firstly, it makes reassembly visible simply by being an assembly of surprising and multicultural people. And secondly, it demonstrates this by recognizing its connection with our brothers and sisters all over the world. And therefore no local church assembly is to think of itself as self-standing or self-sufficient. They are never to forget that they are 'called to be holy, *together with* all those everywhere who call on the name of our LORD Jesus Christ' (1 Cor. 1:2). Those dispersed assemblies have a spiritual unity in Christ that will one day be visible for all to see.

And it is partially visible now. One Christian author comments that, 'If the whole of Britain became Christian tomorrow, the country would remain a vibrantly multicultural society.'[3] This is one of the wonderful things about being a Christian. Incidentally, it is both ironic and sad when liberal white British people persist in thinking of Christianity as a white religion, when its origins were non-white and its global growth is overwhelmingly African, Asian and South American rather than European or North American. Some years ago when I and some of my fellow school-governors opposed the appointment of a practising Muslim to a class teacher position in a church school, we were accused of being racist, on the supposed grounds that Christianity is a white religion. It is not.

The world is breaking apart at every level. Marriages and families creak under all sorts of strains; nations are riven by tribe, race, class or culture. At every level the world is characterised by fragmentation rather than integration. But the local Christian church is to be a sign that alongside this disintegration there is another and supernatural process taking place, of integration, of assembly. And this assembly happens by the preached word of his grace. This is a great theme, the connection between preaching and assembly, between what we toil at as we 'labour in preaching and teaching' (1 Tim. 5:17 ESV), and the rebuilding of a broken world. When I want to help society after the stabbing of our local teenager, in fact, contrary to what we might expect, preaching and training preachers may be the very best thing I can do. For the preaching of the voice of the one God who holds the world together is the only force that can ultimately reunite a world of fragmented voices.

Finally, I want to explore four practical applications of the theological truths about the assembly that we have been considering.

---

3.   Jonathan Chaplin, 'Has Multiculturalism Had Its Day? Towards a Christian Assessment' in *Ethics in Brief* Spring 2008 (Vol.12 No.6)

C. Four Practical Applications, relating the assembly to preaching

1. *The significance of gathering: We gather to hear the word, because our gathering is itself significant*

In Deuteronomy 4:10 the LORD says to Moses, 'Assemble the people before me to hear my words.' Those of us soaked in Western individualistic culture want to read this instruction as follows. This, we want to say, is a functional instruction. The reason for the assembly was in order to facilitate the hearing. The hearing is primary, the goal; the assembly is simply a means to that end, the only means possible in that culture. If we can now find ways to do the hearing without the assembling, so much the less trouble for us. This is how we want to read it. They had to assemble because in those days unless they assembled they would not physically be able to hear God's spokesman proclaim the word. Ah, but since Gutenberg invented the printing press, and since translators got to work, the word is widely available in printed form in many languages; so all I now need to do is to get hold of a Bible in my language and then read it on my own. Indeed, since the invention of voice recording, I can play myself a recording of a sermon, sitting in my room on my own. I can sit with my iPod on a train or a bus. It may not make me dance like the iPod adverts, but I can hear the word. Now I can listen to the word in a bubble of comfortable isolation without having to travel or relate to other people.

That is to say, in a hundred different ways, I can now achieve the object of listening to the word of God without physically gathering with the people of God. If we translate Deuteronomy 4:10 using 'dynamic equivalence', we want to write it as, 'Use whatever technology you like to make sure they hear my words.' That is, we may translate 'gather' or 'assemble' by some word prefixed by tele-, a pseudo-gathering managed by technological wizardry even though our bodies are still scattered at a distance. We can substitute technological wizardry for bodily assembly.

Or, in a softer variant of this objection, 'If you really insist I must gather, well then, I can meet quite comfortably one to one with a Christian friend and we can read and speak about our Bibles together. Or, if you tiresomely say that two is too few, well then, I can meet with a small group of people I like and we can study and discuss our Bibles together. I enjoy discussion. I find it congenial and engaging. Why must you insist that I should also gather with the whole local church? That does not sit well with my culture or my preferences. I may gather like that from time to time to please you; but my core activity will be the private Bible reading, the one-to-one or the small group. That will be where my primary loyalty lies, perhaps to a one-to-one Bible meeting or a cell group in a cell church, where my primary loyalty is to the cell, or to a so-called "youth church" where I gather with people like me.' As some might have suggested in the 1st Century to Paul, it would be more comfortable to have one group for Jews and another for Gentiles. Why do we need to assemble all together?

But we do not gather just in order to hear; we gather because gathering is important. Gathering is what Jesus does. The time when the whole local church gathers is a foretaste of the time when all redeemed humanity will gather. We could scrap Bible study groups and still be a church (an impoverished church, perhaps, but still a church); but if we fail to gather together in our main meetings under the preached word of God, we cease to be a church.

2.   *The significance of preaching for the gathering: Only the word of grace gathers and keeps unlikely people together*

How is the world to be reassembled? Not by technology. Years ago I worked briefly in the telecommunications industry. And as a zealous young Christian I remember trying to persuade my summer camp leader that this was a good place for a Christian to work because telecommunications would bring people together. I blush to remember my naïve foolishness. I saw some research recently that shows, ironically, that the mobile phone revolution is actually diminishing and weakening our interactions with those unlike us. We are better connected than ever, but we are connected to those like us, to those we choose, to friends and family, but not to strangers, not to the person unlike us who never makes it to our contacts list, but to whom we will relate by grace in a church. Even telecommunications may reduce, rather than increase, human mixing. We no longer need physically to be present with people in an office or meeting; instead we have virtual meetings.[4]

How is the world to be reassembled? Not by technology. And not by force. In 2008 the British Museum brought some of the famous Terracotta Army figures from China to London.[5] In the exhibition they told some of the fascinating history of the Emperor Qin Shihuang who unified China in 221 B.C. It was an amazing story of military technology and organisational brilliance – and brute force. How did he unify China? By an army of 700,000 slave soldiers and labourers, most of whom died. And he claimed, in a remarkable inscription in 219 B.C., 'The August Divine Emperor has unified cosmic power over the universe.' He recognised that putting the world together is what gods try to do. And because he had done it, he claimed to be God. But he did it by force. And so the moment he died the whole thing fell apart, like Alexander the Great's empire a century earlier in the West. How is the world to be reassembled? Not by force, but only by grace.

How is the world to be reassembled? Not by technology; not by force; not even by natural human affection. I remember talking rather hesitantly to a hairdresser about Jesus while he was cutting my hair (it has always seemed to me a risky thing to talk to someone wielding a knife in such close proximity, especially when you might offend him). He turned out to be a Buddhist. We got to talking about love, and he told me with some confidence that 'we (Buddhists) have the love within ourselves'. It is an attractive idea, or it would be if it were true. But human beings do not have within themselves the kind of love that can reassemble a broken world.

---

4. *The Economist* April 12th 2008 p. 16
5. British Museum, London, special exhibition *The last emperor* 2008

By nature people do assemble; they get together for all sorts of reasons. It is not true that humanity is simply scattered, each on his own. There are all sorts of assemblies in a scattered and disintegrating world. But the golden rule is that they are gatherings of like with like. Like-minded people will always gather. But when they gather, it is a club, united by some common interest. The people who gather come together because they have something in common. Perhaps they are the kind of people who would quite naturally go on holiday together. By nature, human community is like taking a random collection of buttons of different colours and sorting them so that like goes with like. All the red buttons in one corner, the brass buttons in another, and so on. Like race with like race (blacks with blacks, pink with pink, yellow with yellow), class with class (white collar with white collar, blue collar with blue collar), education with education (graduates with graduates), language with language, and so on.

In Rudyard Kipling's poem,

> Mother, Father, and me,
> Sister, and Auntie say,
> People like Us are 'We'
> And everyone else is 'They'
> And They live over the sea,
> While We live over the way,
> But – would you believe it? – They look upon We
> As only a sort of They![6]

I was reading a report recently which showed that American society is becoming more and more divided. The report was on the phenomenon known as 'clustering', by which people tend to gravitate to live in areas where there are people who share their views. In particular, Republicans are increasingly likely to live in overwhelmingly Republican areas, and Democrats in largely

---

6.   Rudyard Kipling, 'We and They' from *Debits and Credits* 1923

Democrat neighbourhoods (and the study showed that this clustering was not only or even mainly for economic reasons). In 1976 Jimmy Carter won the presidency with 50.1 per cent of the popular vote. And yet 26.8 per cent of Americans were in 'landslide' counties, in which Carter either won or lost by more than 20 percentage points. That is to say, roughly a quarter of Americans lived in overwhelmingly Republican or Democrat counties. In the dead-heat election of 2000, 45.3 per cent of Americans lived in 'landslide' counties, and by 2004 it was 48.3 per cent. That is to say, the proportion of Americans who have chosen to live in neighbourhoods that are predominantly inhabited by people who share their own views has grown over the past three decades from a quarter to a half.[7]

Our natural tendency is to seek out an assembly of people like us. Because of course it is more comfortable, and we'll be able to get along without needing the preached word of grace, which is so humbling.

How is the world to be reassembled? Neither by technology nor by force, nor by human affection. And not by religion.

Natural assemblies can morph into religious assemblies. For example, in scripture there is the hostile assembly of Korah and others who 'came as a group (ESV "assembled themselves together") against Moses and Aaron' (Num. 16:3). There is the hostile assembly of Psalm 2, in which the powers on earth gather together against the LORD and his Christ. That hostile assembly reconstituted when Herod and Pontius Pilate together with the Gentiles and the people of Israel gathered together against Jesus (Acts 4:27). And it reconstituted again in Acts 4 when the rulers and elders and scribes, with Annas the high priest and Caiaphas and John and Alexander and all the high-priestly family gathered together in Jerusalem against the apostles (Acts 4:5f.) This kind of assembly is like predators gathering to the prey. We see this in the authoritarian liberalism

---

7.   'The Big Sort', in *The Economist* 21st June 2008

in some parts of the Anglican Communion today, notably perhaps in New Westminster in Canada.

Then there is the empty assembly, the solemn assemblies that look like the people of God but aren't because there's no justice, no godliness, assemblies that God hates (Amos 5:21), having a form of godliness but denying its power (2 Tim. 3:5). This is the kind of pseudo-church that lures people to its assembly like siren voices onto the rocks. We are drawn to this kind of assembly like moths to a trap. It is more dangerous than paganism.

Then there are superficial assemblies, such as the crowds that surrounded Jesus early in his ministry, drawn by the excitement of the miracles, an evanescent phenomenon, with a spiritual life like a firework – bright today, gone tomorrow.

A church can very easily become any of these things – superficial, empty, even hostile to God.

So how is the world to be reassembled? Not by technology. Not by force. Not by natural human affection. Not by religion. But only by grace.

Only the preached word of Christ, the word of grace preached again and again and again, pressed home with passion and engagement, only that word will create God's assembly to rebuild a broken world. It has been said that the church is the crater formed by the impact of the word of God (Karl Barth);[8] or that 'the scriptures are God's voice, the church is his echo' (John Donne).[9] Those are vivid pictures. But it is perhaps more scriptural to say that the church is the living organism conceived, shaped and grown by the seed of the word of God within (cf. James 1:18, 21; 1 Pet. 1:23). The church's DNA is the DNA of the preached word of God. And by that word Jesus gathers unlikely people.

When Christ builds his church, his *qahal*, his *ecclesia*, his assembly, he must first humble pride. Nothing so humbles

---

8. Karl Barth, *The Epistle to the Romans* (London: Oxford University Press, 1933), p. 36f.
9. quoted in Peter Adam, *Hearing God's Words* (IVP Apollos, 2004), p. 13

pride as the word of his grace, which makes us debtors to mercy alone. We enter the church with nothing in our hands, but simply clinging to the cross. Only the word of his grace will do that in us, by the power and mercy of God. Supremely that is done by the public proclamation of that word in preaching. What the preaching of grace does is to gather a people who join their assembly humbled under grace. Our identity is defined not by our achievement but by redemption, not by what we have done, but by what has been done for us, just as Israel was defined as those who were slaves in Egypt and had been redeemed with a strong hand and a mighty arm.

There is something deeply attractive about a people gathered by grace. Dead assemblies, empty assemblies where there is the outward show of religion but no power of grace, will look over the fence at a real assembly of grace and become jealous (which is Paul's great hope and strategy in Rom. 11). But it only happens when those people are gathered by the proclamation of grace.

Only the word of grace keeps unlikely people together. 'Now I commit you to God', says Paul to the Ephesian elders (Acts 20:32), 'and to the word of his grace, which can build you up and give you an inheritance among all those who are sanctified.' That inheritance language (as in Acts 26:18; Eph. 1:14; Col. 1:12, 3:24) picks up promised land language; the promised land of Deuteronomy is the land they would inherit (e.g. Deut. 1:38). This land is a scale model and signpost to the new creation. But how are we to be 'built up' corporately as a reassembled people? Answer: by 'the word of his grace'. Why is this? Because only the word of his grace knocks down our pride. And only when our pride is continually knocked down can we together corporately be built up. (So, for example, it is the regular reading of the law that stops the King being lifted up above his brothers, in Deut. 17:18-20.)

That is to say, only a church where grace is preached repeatedly and forcefully will be preserved from degenerating into a club. Just as a variegated shrub can revert into one with a single colour of leaf, so a church can so easily revert to being mono-cultural. We must be realistic about this. We must not beat ourselves because our churches are not wonderfully and ideally multi-cultural. We live in a broken world, and therefore Jesus starts church-building using broken materials. Our churches are bound to reflect in some way the divisions within our society, if only at the lowest level the social differences in different localities. The wonder is not that our churches are not perfect. The wonder is that they are beginning to bring together unlikely people, that they are pulling against the culture that keeps one race together or one class together or one type of person together.

This movement from homogeneity to heterogeneity cannot be engineered by positive discrimination (the token different person) or by hectoring or lecturing ('You rotten old middle-class Christians ought to be more multicultural'). It will only be created supernaturally by the preached word of grace in Jesus Christ.

The word of sovereign grace, preached and preached and preached again, is the necessary condition for the shaping of a people of grace, who alone can reassemble a broken world. All churches will tend to revert from grace to being a homogeneous club. Grace is fragile, because grace humbles human pride. A church without the public preaching of grace at its heart will always slip away from grace. A church with grace as its theme tune in preaching will be held to grace.

3. The word of grace shapes us together

When we listen together we are accountable to one another for our response. Hearing while gathered is significantly different and better than hearing alone. My point now is to do with the chemistry and dynamics of a physical gathering. When I read my Bible on my own (which is a good thing to do!), it is all too easy for my thoughts to drift, my eye to stray from the page, my heart to be inattentive to the word. If I sit and listen to a recording of a sermon, it is all too easy to hit the 'Stop' button, either actually or metaphorically as my attention 'switches off'.

When I gather with my brothers and sisters to hear the word preached, it is still possible to hit the 'Off' button. I can look out of the window; I can read Wesley's instructions for congregational singing in *Christian Hymns*; I can read the 39 Articles at the end of the Book of Common Prayer; I can doodle; I can day-dream. But it is not quite so easy. For I have sitting around me brothers and sisters who might notice; and I would hate to be seen to be inattentive. And I have sitting around me brothers and sisters who may talk to me afterwards about the sermon; and it will be embarrassing if I have no idea what it was about.

Further, when we listen together, you know what word I have heard, and I know what word you have heard. I've heard it. You know I've heard it. I know that you know I've heard it! And you expect and hope that I will respond appropriately to that word, just as I expect and hope that you will do the same. We are accountable to one another for our response, and this stirs us up and encourages us to respond as we know we ought.

Indeed, the weekly gatherings of the local church to hear the preached word should be understood as the primary dynamic and driving force of church life, alongside the gatherings for corporate prayer. All the other contexts in which Bibles are opened, read or discussed, have a supportive rather than a normative role in church life. Or, to put it bluntly, a church will be a church so long as it gathers to hear the word, even if none of its members meets in small groups or even reads the Bible on their own! And conversely, if they wilfully neglect the gathering of the church under the preached word they are not properly a church, even if they do all these other things. The writer to the Hebrews does not tell them, 'Don't neglect your Quiet Time'; he says, 'Let us not give up meeting together' (Heb. 10:25), because that's where they sit together under the preached word of God.

When we listen together, we respond together. The word of God is generally addressed to the people of God corporately, and to individuals only as members of that corporate body. This is disguised in modern English translations, where we cannot tell, for example, whether "you" is "you (singular)" or "you (plural)". It is plural much more than it is singular. The purpose of the word of God is to create, shape, and sustain the people of God. And the local expression of the people of God is the local church. The size of the local church is not the point; a local church can be a very small gathering (as it often is in many parts of the world). But a house group or Bible study group is not in general a local church, with properly ordered leadership who admit newcomers to membership, who administer discipline, who share the LORD's Supper as a fellowship existing as a local church unit.

For this reason, the assembly of the whole local church under the preached word ought to have pride of place in our thinking as the defining context of church. We are to ask, 'What is God saying to *us*?' before we ask, 'What is God saying to *me*?' All the other contexts in which we hear the word are important and beneficial. It is good, very good, that we read our Bibles on our own or that we read the Bible with one another in pairs or small groups. These things serve to reinforce the spiritual hunger and attentiveness of the fellowship, so that when we gather together to hear the word preached, our hearts are eager and ready humbly to sit under his mighty hand. But it is the corporate gathering of the fellowship which defines and shapes the church.

The word of grace is to be performed corporately and not just interpreted individually.

We tend to think that Bible interpretation is 'deciding what the Bible means'. In our western culture we naturally assume this is an individual endeavour, done privately in the study. The first step is to take on board that Bible interpretation is a corporate endeavour. We need one another, not least to help us see our blind spots. And in particular we need brothers and sisters from different cultures to help us see this. Otherwise we may all agree on an interpretation because we share the same blind spot.

But the point I have only recently begun to grasp is that Bible *interpretation* isn't really the point. The point of the Bible is to shape a people under grace who will be people of grace. That is to say, the goal of the Bible is Bible performance, not Bible interpretation. The Bible is not there to be interpreted; it is there to be performed, and performed by a people corporately. Dietrich Bonhoeffer put it like this: 'The essence of the church is not to practise theology but to *believe* and *obey* the word of God.'[10]

Our challenge is not simply to understand the word we hear preached but to do it. Our business is not Bible interpretation but Bible performance.[11] We need to be a community who interpret the word; but the kind of interpretation we are to aim at is much more than agreeing what it means. We are to interpret the word in the sense of becoming a living visible interpretation of the word, a community in which the word of Christ is lived out and made concrete. We will only do this if we understand that our gatherings as whole local churches under the preached word are the defining context for church.

I think we may be helped here when we remember that a great chunk of Deuteronomy is instruction given to shape a people under grace. Of course these laws need to be read through the prism of Jesus Christ in ways appropriate to the new covenant. But the point is this: people under grace need to behave and live together as people of grace. Deuteronomy shows this quite unselfconsciously from time to time. For example in Deuteronomy 10:19, in the context of exhortation

---

10.   Dietrich Bonhoeffer, *Reflections on the Bible: human word and word of God* (tr.M.Eugene Boring. Hendrikson, 2004), p. 89, quoted in Peter Adam, *Written for Us: Receiving God's Words* (IVP, 2008), p. 162f.

11.   Kevin J.Vanhoozer, *The Drama of Doctrine* (Westminster: John Knox Press, 2005)

to loyalty to the LORD, Moses suddenly slips in, 'And you are to love those who are aliens, for you yourselves were aliens in Egypt.' We might paraphrase this, 'and by the way, love the outsider, for you were outsiders living in a land of slavery and the LORD redeemed you. You received grace; be people of overflowing grace to others.' We see this illustrated in Deuteronomy 15:7-11, where the underlying logic is this: God has given you the land generously, and so you must be generous in sharing with others.

The purpose of preaching is not preaching. Preaching is not an end in itself. We do not preach so that people will go away saying, 'That was good preaching.' The purpose of preaching is performance – not the performance of the preacher but the corporate performance of the whole assembly whose lives and relationships are shaped by the preached word of grace. Therefore in our preaching we must not neglect practical instruction about ethics, how to behave, how to live as people under grace.

4. God reaches the world by shaping the church by the preached word.
We reach the world by preaching to the church. My final point is this: the world watches the church, and therefore the shape of the church is of great importance for the destiny of a watching world. The assembly is to be a place with open borders; not Israel in an isolation ward, but Israel watched by the world. Israel is to exist 'in the sight of the peoples' (Deut. 4:6 ESV). We might say they are to be a kind of Show House of God's gracious dealings with a people. As Calvin put it, 'a stage had been erected before other nations, whereon the nobility of that one people would be conspicuous.'[12]

The Assembly of Israel was never completely closed, even in Old Testament times. The mere fact that laws have to be stated restricting, for example, whether Moabites or Edomites

---

12. Calvin, *Commentary on Deuteronomy* ad. loc

can or cannot enter the Assembly means that the possibility of a foreigner coming in was always there (Deut. 23:1-8). Just as Israel had immigrants, visiting foreigners, and traders coming in and out, so the church has open borders.

The most vivid example of this in Deuteronomy is in Deuteronomy 4:6-8, 'Observe (the laws) carefully, for this will show your wisdom and understanding to the nations, who will hear about all these decrees and say, "Surely this great nation is a wise and understanding people." What other nation is so great as to have their gods near them the way the LORD our God is near us whenever we pray to him? And what other nation is so great as to have such righteous decrees and laws as this body of laws I am setting before you today?'

As the people shaped by redeeming grace learn to do the laws of grace, so they become wise. That is to say, they learn how to live in the real world. And the world watches. And the world says, 'Surely this great nation is a wise and understanding people.' It is clear and evident that they are close to God because their laws and lives are shaped by righteousness. And although Moses does not spell it out, the implication surely is that some of them will knock on the doors of the assembly of Israel and ask admittance, as Ruth the Moabitess did in a later age.

The preached instruction of God was to shape a people of wisdom, who understood reality and so knew how to live in the world. That was why in Deuteronomy 1:9-18 they needed wise judges and local officials (vv. 13, 15 'Choose some wise, understanding and respected men … So I took the leading men of your tribes, wise and respected men …'). They would need to be so shaped by the gracious law of God that they could make godly decisions in new circumstances. And then the world would see that this people were close to God. The world was to be reached through the wise and righteous life of Israel, shaped under grace.

By and large we who are preachers do not reach the world with the word. Mostly the world will not listen to the word. Christ shapes his church with the word, and the church reaches the world. 'If a preacher is to act on the world he must, as a rule, do it through his church…He is to preach to the church from the word, so that with the church he may preach the gospel to the world.'[13] As Paul puts it in Ephesians, the foundation work of the apostles and prophets, and the ongoing work of the evangelists and pastor-teachers, is 'to prepare God's people for works of service', Ephesians 4:11, 12. This was Jesus' own strategy in his ministry, to shape a group of disciples in Israel so that from that group he could preach to the world. The purpose of the preached word of God is to shape the people of God so that the world will see the light of God's grace. The church is to be grace made concrete, what Lesslie Newbigin called 'the hermeneutic of the gospel.'[14] And so the movement is not direct from the word to the world; it is from the word to the world via the church. The preached word week by week shapes the church; and the church reaches the world.

This emphasis is one of the great strengths of Tim Chester and Steve Timmis's stimulating book *Total Church: A radical reshaping around gospel and community.*[15] Chester and Timmis want us to recapture the priority of the local church community as the concrete expression of the gospel. They are right to do so (even though I do not share their lack of enthusiasm for preaching), for the world will in general be reached through the church.

I think this means that the church is the proper and normal context for evangelism. A student came up to me after a meeting and said, 'We're told that the church is the place to be built up in our faith, and equipped, and then we go out to evangelize as individual Christians. But I am beginning to see that evangelism is to be done corporately.' We often say that our non-Christian friends will probably not read the Bible, but they will read our lives. This is true. But what this student had begun to grasp, and I have begun to grasp, is this: they will

---

13. P.T. Forsyth, *Positive Preaching and the Modern Mind* (3rd Edition. London: Independent Press, 1949), pp. 52, 53

14. Lesslie Newbigin, *The Gospel in a Pluralist Society* (SPCK, 1989) pp. 222-233

15. Tim Chester and Steve Timmis, *Total Church* (IVP, 2007)

not just read our lives as individuals; they will read our lives in relationship, and in particular as we relate together as Christian brothers and sisters. They will see in the way the church relates and lives together as a community shaped by grace the visible evidence of the existence and the character of the invisible God. They won't just watch the individual Christian. They will see in Christians together a way of relating which is clearly supernatural. They will see forgiveness, forbearance, patience and practical love.

Chester and Timmis argue this movingly, and include this testimony from a Chinese non-Christian man. He told a Christian friend that he had done a Bible course when he first came to the UK, but had understood almost none of it. A year later, he wants to study the Bible again. Why? Because he has seen and watched the lives of Christians as they relate to one another and others in the world.[16] There are distinctives in them that have made him say, as in Deuteronomy 4:6-8, 'That's a wise people, a people close to God, if there is a God. I want to find out more.'

The wisdom and love of the people shaped by the preaching of grace will overflow to others. In his book *Promoting the Gospel* John Dickson tells the story of Kathy. When Kathy was six her mother, who was not a Christian, fell ill with cancer. Out of the blue, the local Baptist church offered to pay for an operation she could not otherwise have afforded. The kindness of that church to the family through that time stayed with Kathy until a full thirty years later she came right through to a clear faith in Jesus Christ.[17]

CONCLUSION

'Gather the people to me', says God to Moses. 'Gather the people to me', says the Father to Jesus as he sends him on his rescue mission to this world. 'Gather more people to me', says

16.   Tim Chester and Steve Timmis, *Total Church* (IVP, 2007), p. 57f.
17.   John Dickson, *Promoting the Gospel* (Sydney: Blue bottle books, 2005), pp. 81-83

Jesus to his people, and perhaps especially to those entrusted with the public preaching of the word, 'for the one who does not gather with me scatters'. He wants us to gather them by his word and to be shaped by his word, because those words of grace will remake a broken world.

I hope that you and I as preachers will be encouraged that the ministry entrusted to us is the primary ministry of the word. It is a ministry given by God to shape a people to reassemble the world. God's strategy for rebuilding a broken world is to create dispersed assemblies shaped by his word of grace. And those dispersed assemblies, straddling divisions of race, class, and culture, and linked with other assemblies all over the world, will be his instruments to bring forgiveness, healing and new life under Christ. What you and I do this Sunday, weak and irrelevant though it may seem, is how a broken world will be reassembled.

Appendix

Give God the Microphone!

Seven Blessings of Consecutive Expository Preaching

When I was newly-ordained my senior minister asked me to interview in church a visitor engaged in some ministry that he wanted the church to know about and pray for. I was to do this using a hand-held radio mic. However he warned me, 'This man is tremendously talkative and we need to keep the interview to its allotted time slot. So, WHATEVER YOU DO, DON'T GIVE HIM THE MICROPHONE!' I therefore stood up at the appointed time, invited this brother to join me, held the microphone as I asked the first question and then clung to it tightly as I held it out in front of him for his answer. All seemed well until, a few seconds into his answer, he said, 'Do you mind if I take that thing (the mic)?' Well, I didn't feel it would be edifying to say 'No' and have a tug of war in front of six hundred people, so I lamely said, 'No, of course not' (through gritted teeth, with a sense of impending doom), surrendered the microphone and the interview overshot its time allocation by a long way. Which is a parable, to which I shall return below.

The theme of this book is the priority of preaching. All preaching must be expository, in the strict sense that we must bring out of scripture what God by his Spirit has breathed into scripture. If we fail to do that, we may be no better than idle dreamers of dreams (cf. Deut. 13:1) and our sermons of no more value than any other human opinions. But while all preaching must be expository, I want in this appendix to commend the blessings of making our preaching diet consist mainly of *consecutive* expository ministry, where we take a Bible book, or section of a book, and work through it in a sermon series. In general I mean by this simply taking consecutive passages and working right through the book. But we may need to modify this approach for very long books such as Isaiah, either by selecting a smaller section (perhaps Isa. 1–5) or by choosing representative passages to help our churches get into the book as a whole.[1]

David Jackman makes the nice comparison between a church and a car. So, to pursue the metaphor, we might put the Bible in the boot or trunk of the car. It is then brought out from time to time and looked at briefly. But it is never seriously examined. Most of us have been to churches like that, where you have to look hard to find a Bible, or a Bible that has more than a 'bit part' in church life. Then we might promote the Bible from the boot to the backseat, a place where – like a backseat driver – it can interfere and be irritating, tiresomely questioning our driving or our directions. But it is still no more than an irritation or a diversion, to be ignored in the hopes that eventually it will shut up and get on with the crossword or sudoku. Then again we might put the Bible in the front passenger seat, a place from which its contribution might be really quite helpful, reading the map, looking at the signposts, putting a CD on to keep us awake, changing the radio channel. But for all that, we are still making the decisions that really matter, how fast to go and in what direction. So what we really need to do in our church life is to put the Bible in the driving seat. For when the Bible is in the driving seat of church life, then God is in the driving seat.

---

1. My book *Out of the Storm: grappling with God in the book of Job* (IVP, 2004) originated in such a series of seven sermons taking us through the whole book of Job

Appendix: Give God the Microphone!

And all our church activities, relationships, diary and meetings are governed, directed, led and controlled by scripture. That is our aim. Consecutive expository preaching ministry helps us move in the right direction for that aim.

When the apostle Peter was reinstated and given the job of being a pastor, Jesus said to him, 'Feed my sheep' (John 21:17). That is what a pastor is, a shepherd, whose job it is to feed the sheep. The great seventeenth century Puritan theologian John Owen wrote, 'The first and principal duty of a pastor is to feed the flock by diligent preaching of the Word. It is a promise relating to the New Testament, that God 'would give unto his church pastors according to his own heart, which should feed them with knowledge and understanding' (Jer. 3:15). This is by preaching or teaching the word, and not otherwise. This feeding is of the essence of the office of a pastor ... The care of preaching the gospel was committed to Peter, and in him to all true pastors of the church, under the name of 'feeding' (John 21:15-17). According to the example of the apostles, they are to free themselves from all encumbrances, that they may give themselves wholly unto the word and prayer (Acts 6:1-4). Their work is to "labour in the word and doctrine" (1 Tim. 5:17), and thereby to feed the flock over which the Holy Ghost has made them overseers (Acts 20)… This work and duty, therefore, as was said, is essential unto the office of a pastor ... Nor is it required only that he preach now and then at his leisure; but that he lay aside all other employments, though lawful, all other duties in the church, as unto such a constant attendance on them as would divert him from this work, that he may give himself unto it ... Without this, no man will be able to give a comfortable account of the pastoral office at the last day.'[2]

I had a curious experience one summer, which brought home to me again how vital is the work of preaching (and of training preachers). I was taking our daughter and a friend

---

2.   John Owen, *Works* XVI: 74f., quoted in J.I. Packer, *Among God's Giants: the Puritan vision of the Christian life* (Kingsway, 1991), p. 372f.

to Thorpe Park, a theme park near London (a kind of glorified adventure playground). The girls were queuing for a terrifying ride with ten loop-the-loops and five barrel rolls, and I – with the wisdom of years – was sitting it out, quietly reading a book on my own (insofar as you can ever be on your own in such places). And then to my surprise a stranger joined me and asked me what church I went to. In England it is curious enough that he should speak to me without being introduced; it is even more curious to start the conversation by asking me what church I belonged to. I think he must have noticed that I was reading a Christian book. We talked, and it turned out he was a Christian too (and a wise one at that, since he was sitting out the same ride while his wife went on it)! At some point in our conversation I told him that I worked for a Bible training course, seeking to help people teach and preach the Bible. At this point he commented slightly wistfully that at his church the sermons are 'more like lifestyle tips' than anything serious from the Bible. This was at a lively, contemporary, growing, supposedly 'evangelical' church. The sheep were coming to church hungry and leaving unfed. In how many other churches are the sheep going home saying they have been given 'lifestyle tips'?

Among those who take the Bible seriously, there are different ways in which we can teach the Bible, varieties of diet for feeding the sheep. There is preaching that takes a doctrinal topic, such as the humanity of Jesus Christ, and tries to tackle that. Or we might preach a series on the Apostles' Creed, looking at fundamental Christian truths systematically. There is preaching that takes an ethical topic, such as abortion or climate change, and seeks to bring the Bible to bear upon it. Or there is preaching that addresses some contemporary issue of controversy in the church or the world. All these can, with care, be done responsibly in a way that is expounding the teaching of the Bible.

But what I want to commend to you as the staple diet of feeding the sheep is none of these, but consecutive expository preaching. I am not suggesting that we ought never to preach topical sermons; I am proposing that the normal regular week by week diet should usually be working through a book of the Bible, and that this is the most nourishing basis for the diet of the sheep (ourselves included). I want therefore to suggest that topical preaching ought to be the exception rather than the rule.

Let me set before you seven blessings of having consecutive expository ministry as the staple diet on the menu of the people of God. I do this, neither because we can prove from scripture that it is the only way to preach, nor because we can show from church history that it ought always to be the norm (although the preaching of Calvin in Geneva and of Chrysostom in Antioch ought to encourage us);[3] I do this, because of the blessings that seem to me to accompany good consecutive expository ministry.

1. CONSECUTIVE EXPOSITORY PREACHING SAFEGUARDS GOD'S AGENDA AGAINST BEING HIJACKED BY OURS

When we do topical preaching we (as it were) hold the microphone in front of God and ask him the questions of our choice. We hold the microphone there just long enough to hear his answers, and then we take it away. We do not want to take the risk of letting him have the microphone; after all, he might want to tell us all sorts of things we may not want to hear. To do consecutive expository preaching gives God the microphone. We hand it over to him and we listen while God tells us what he wants us to hear. He sets the agenda for our teaching and our learning. Let us give God the microphone.

I want to exorcise three demons. They are called Relevance, Entertainment, and Immediacy. Let me introduce you to them.

---

3.   see T.H.L. Parker, *Calvin's Preaching* (Edinburgh: T & T Clark, 1992) and J.N.D. Kelly, *Golden Mouth: The Story of John Chrysostom* (Cornell University Press, 1995) (biography of John Chrysostom).

(a) Relevance

Relevance is a clever demon. He says, 'When you preach, you must be relevant to your people. What point is there in preaching that is irrelevant, that does not engage with people? Such preaching floats around up in the air, but never lands. No, you must make sure your preaching is relevant.' So for this demon, the worst thing you can say as you leave church is, 'The sermon was irrelevant.'

Well, he's right, in a sense. But the clever thing about the demon Relevance is what he does not say. The subtext is this: How do we define what is relevant? Who decides what is relevant? Answer: the hearers do! What Relevance means is that I must scratch *where they itch*. And therefore my method is the method of the contemporary politician. I must find out where they are itching. So I gather a Focus Group, I take an opinion poll, I build up a picture of the issues bugging people. And this forms my agenda, which I address in my topical preaching. My preaching agenda is their itching agenda. They come to me as patients with their presenting symptoms, perhaps of anxiety, discomfort, low self-esteem or loneliness. And as their spiritual doctor I prescribe remedies for their perceived ills.

The problem – as every good doctor knows – is that the patients' perceived ills, their presenting symptoms, their itches, may mask a deeper but unperceived illness. And the only one who knows the deeper illness is the God who made us. The Bible is the written expression of God's agenda, the word of the God who made us. It expresses his purposes, his plans; it centres on him, not on us, and speaks to us only as we relate to him. To preach expositorily through a Bible book is to trust that the agenda of God is the right, the deepest, the best agenda.

Let me give you an example. A trainee preacher was giving a short exposition to a class of trainee preachers on 1 Thessalonians 5:12-13 (part of a series working through 1 Thessalonians). He knew as he read it that it is an apostolic instruction to Christians to respect and esteem highly those over them in the Lord. 'Ah,' whispered Relevance in his ear,

Appendix: Give God the Microphone!

'but you are speaking to men and women on a Bible-teaching training course. Your fellow-students are – for the most part – engaged in or preparing for Bible-teaching ministry. It is not relevant to tell them to respect those over them in the Lord; it is more a case of them being over various others in the Lord. So he looked for something 'relevant' to Bible teachers in the verses, and found it in the little comment Paul makes when he describes Bible teachers as 'those who work hard among you'. His teaching point was that Bible teachers ought to work hard. Well, we ought. But it was not the main point of the verses, and he ought to have trusted God's agenda and taught us what the verses teach. He admitted to me later that it was a misuse of scripture. He had failed to trust the agenda of God.

(b) Entertainment

The demon 'Entertainment' is sovereign in much of western culture. Neil Postman has commented perceptively on it in his provocative book, *Amusing ourselves to Death*.[4] Entertainment whispers in our ear, 'The most terrible thing anyone can say about a sermon is, "That was *boring*." You must entertain, you must tell jokes, build up a fund of good anecdotes, tickle your hearers' ears with interest and laughter.'

And so when we read the next passage in our sermon series, on a Monday, and it just seems a bit dull, Entertainment says, 'Find something in the passage that links with something interesting. Bounce off the passage, like a trampoline, up into something more exciting. In his *Lectures to his Students* the great 19th Century Baptist preacher Charles Spurgeon calls it using the passage as a mounting block from which to climb up onto our winged horse Pegasus, on which we can fly where we will, leaving the boring passage well behind. He writes, 'Some brethren have done with their text as soon as they have read it. Having paid all due honour to that particular passage by announcing it, they

---

4.   Neil Postman, *Amusing ourselves to Death: Public Discourse in the Age of Show Business* (Methuen, 1985)

feel no necessity further to refer to it. They touch their hats, as it were, to that part of Scripture, and pass on to fresh fields and pastures new. Why do such men take a text at all? Why limit their own glorious liberty? Why make Scripture a horsing-block [i.e. a mounting block] by which to mount upon their unbridled Pegasus? Surely the words of inspiration were never meant to be boothooks to help a Talkative to draw on his seven-leagued boots in which to leap from pole to pole.'[5]

When we let God set the agenda, we are released from the slavery of the stage, the slavery to feel that we simply must entertain. Instead we trust that God will hold the attention of all in whom he is at work, and towards whom he has decided to work in grace. This is not to say that we cultivate dreary preaching; it is to say that the content of our preaching is set not by the demands of entertainment, but by the agenda God has set in the books of the Bible.

(c) Immediacy

The demon 'Immediacy' says, 'People have come to hear your sermon because they want God to speak to them now. They do not want to hear about God speaking in the past. They want to hear God now. You must speak to them a word which touches them now. How wonderful when someone says on the way out, "You know, that sermon was just right for me *now*."'

But this is to misunderstand the nature of scripture. Week after week I need to hear the word of God expounded, not because each week by some divine magic it exactly corresponds with my present needs, but because it is God's instrument to shape, fashion and mould me into the image of Christ. For example, I remember having to preach on the final section of Romans 8 one Sunday (as part of a consecutive series). This passage speaks to suffering Christians who feel like the psalmist in Psalm 44, like sheep in the queue for the abattoir. I guessed (correctly, I think) that most people in the church I served did

---

5.   C.H. Spurgeon, *Lectures to my students* (London: Marshall, Morgan and Scott, 1954), p. 72-3

not feel like that. Mostly they were not being persecuted, at least not with anything approaching that intensity. So the demon 'Immediacy' says to me, 'You must modify this passage so that it speaks to them now.' But God says, 'This is my agenda, for them to hear these truths, so that they are shaped by them. Then when the time of trial comes, they will have proper expectations of the normal Christian life and a right confidence in my unbreakable love in Christ.' We must trust God to set the agenda, and give God the microphone.

So let us exorcise the demons of Relevance, Entertainment and Immediacy, and have the confidence to preach through Bible books week by week. The God who then sets our agenda is a much better judge of what we actually need to hear. No other model of preaching guards us so well against hijacking the sermon by our own human agendas, because only consecutive exposition forces us to take seriously the passage before us, whether or not it seems relevant, entertaining, or the passage for now.

2. CONSECUTIVE EXPOSITORY PREACHING MAKES IT HARDER FOR US TO ABUSE THE BIBLE BY READING IT OUT OF CONTEXT.
We often say that a text without a context is a pretext. People sometimes say, 'You can make the Bible mean anything you want.' And it is quite true. What a text means is what it means in its context. And only when it is read responsibly in context is its meaning correctly discerned.

Somebody lent me once a book commending certain practices of quiet meditation in prayer. It quoted in support Psalm 34:14b, 'Seek peace and pursue it.' So, they said, we must find quiet places to pray and quieten our hearts, and so on. Well, that may be no bad thing to do. But it is not what this verse means. This verse is not saying we must seek quietness and inner calm that we may meditate. The peace that we are to seek here is not an inner sense of calm, but a social and relational harmony, peace rather than war between people. To seek peace is to turn from evil (v. 14a) and act in such a way as to promote peace in a society or community or family. What this writer did was to press-gang a verse of the Bible into the service of their own agenda. This is a terrible and dangerous thing to do with the word of God; we must not do it.

Now it is possible to refer to various verses in a sermon and responsibly and carefully to put each one of them in its proper context, to make sure we understand and read each verse properly. It is possible. When people write systematic theologies, they have to try to do that. And when people give a doctrinal or topical sermon, they ought to do that. But it is difficult. It is difficult and demanding for the teacher; and it is very difficult for the hearers. For the hearers it is like being on a whistle-stop tour. The helicopter comes down briefly in Exodus; we have a quick look around. And then, before we know what has hit us, we have taken off and seconds later we have landed perhaps in Revelation. And then to Luke's Gospel. And so on. It is bewildering, even if our guide is being responsible and careful.

One of the great blessings of a consecutive expository series is that we may take our hearers to the book we are studying, get them firmly grounded in it, and then quietly walk through it. We relate the different parts of the book to one another, so as to build up a far clearer and more accurate understanding of the message of the book as a whole, and of each part within the whole. This is both easier for the hearers and for the preacher. Those who preach consecutive series know how very difficult it is to have to preach a one-off sermon as a visitor in somebody else's series. For we have not only to prepare the passage allocated to us; we ought also to familiarize ourselves with the book as a whole.

So consecutive Bible exposition helps us understand the Bible in its contexts and therefore understand it correctly, and not to abuse the word of God by twisting it to mean something other than what God has made it mean.

Appendix: Give God the Microphone!

3. CONSECUTIVE EXPOSITORY PREACHING DILUTES THE SELECTIVITY OF THE PREACHER

My heart sinks when I am asked to preach a topical sermon. Someone writes and says, 'Please will you preach on the topic of Christian assurance?' Help! What must I do? I ransack my mental map of the Bible trying to forage from it anything that might be relevant. I only have limited time, so I cannot systematically read the Bible through from end to end. So what happens? I pick the bits of the Bible that I happen to know and love that might bear on this subject. And I try to put them in some coherent order and give the talk. I may also enlist some help from reference books.

But all the while the nagging thought in the back of my mind says, 'Christopher, how can you be sure you haven't missed some vital part of the Bible's teaching in this area? Or how can you know you have got the proper balance in scripture's teaching?' Answer: I can't be sure. What I do know is that my talk is likely to reflect my own partial and inadequate knowledge of the Bible, my own prejudices, the bees currently buzzing in my bonnet and my favourite hobby-horses. I hate having to make my own selection of Bible texts like this, because I know that my Bible knowledge is so partial and my selectivity is deeply flawed.

But when I tackle a consecutive exposition, I know what I have to do. Whether I like it or not, whether I am familiar with it or not, I know that I must read and re-read and pray and work and worry away at this week's passage, like a dog at a bone, seeking to preach what this passage says and not what I happen to want to preach about.

Now I realise that those who plan teaching series still have to choose what expository series they tackle. That is their responsibility. They have to select, for example, Matthew 8-10 this season and Exodus next. They ought to try to maintain an overall balance to seek to cover the whole counsel of God – a balance of gospels, epistles and Old Testament, for example.

But they cannot avoid choosing. We cannot entirely avoid the need for selectivity. But at least, having chosen the book, then they have to tackle the whole book, whether or not they like it.

This also means that we have to preach difficult and unpopular topics, simply because they come up in our series. When preaching a series of sermons from the block of Jesus' teaching that is Matthew 18, I inevitably had to devote a sermon to the subject of excommunication (Matt. 18:15-20). I am not aware of any topical series which I would have chosen to include the topic of excommunication. We would not expect it to boost the numbers attending on that particular Sunday and we might be reluctant to encourage our congregations to invite their friends ('Would you like to come to church with me this Sunday to hear a sermon on excommunication?' 'Yes, I'd love to come. Nothing fascinates me more.') But when we preach through Matthew 18 we have to cover it. And that's a good thing, because God has put it there. A minister who preaches through 1 Timothy will have to tackle Paul's unpopular and un-P.C. teaching about the complementary roles of men and women in church (1 Tim. 2:8-15), and to do so in its context. The congregation need not suspect him of having picked the topic to get at them. He tackles the second half of 1 Timothy 2 because last week he tackled the first half.

So here is a third blessing. Consecutive exposition dilutes the selectivity of the preacher. And in this way too it safeguards the agenda of God.

These first three blessings are perhaps a little negative. They are concerned with guarding us against hijacking the Bible to our own ends. We turn now to four very positive blessings.

4. CONSECUTIVE EXPOSITORY PREACHING KEEPS THE CONTENT
   OF THE SERMON FRESH AND SURPRISING
There are some preachers for whom you know in advance what they are going to say. If their Bible passage seems to be at least vaguely about prayer, you will get their standard prayer talk.

Appendix: Give God the Microphone!

Choose another passage that touches on prayer, and you will get the same sermon again. Or it may even be more reductionist than that. Some ministers will almost invariably end up saying something like, (a) we are sinners, (b) we need a Saviour, (c) Jesus is that Saviour because he died for us on the Cross, and so (d) we ought to repent and trust in him. Well, there are worse things they might say! And it's all true. But if that was all there was to say, we may well ask why God chose to give us the whole Bible. It is excellent stuff, in a way. But it feels very much the same week after week. The preacher leaves the particularities of the passage behind and jumps off into his doctrinal framework and preaches that. The result is a truncated gospel, a dumbed–down, flattened, two-dimensional word of God.

The gospel is fuller and richer than those truncated versions. Every passage in the Bible is there because it contributes something unique to God's revelation. And when a preacher asks himself, 'What does *this passage* contribute? Why is this truth told in this way by this passage to these hearers?' then there is a sense of healthy surprise and freshness in the preaching. It is always the same gospel, but never exactly the same sermon.

Consecutive exposition encourages us to ask of each passage in turn, 'What does this passage contribute to the full revelation of God? What do we learn here that we do not perhaps learn, or not learn in the same way, elsewhere in the Bible? One of the reasons I love tackling a consecutive expository series is that I keep learning. If I have to give a topical talk, I have to ransack the resources of my past Bible knowledge, collect suitable material and put it into order. But when I tackle a Bible book, I am constantly learning, being surprised and challenged. When I first preached Job, it changed me. When I teach Romans, I am never the same person at the end as I was when I started. Nor will I be when I teach it again, because – God willing – I will continue to be surprised and to learn. This freshness is a great secret of authentic ministry and a blessing for long-term discipleship.

5. CONSECUTIVE EXPOSITORY PREACHING MAKES FOR VARIETY IN THE STYLE OF THE SERMON

The fifth blessing is closely related to the fourth. If the fourth is about freshness of *content*, the fifth is about freshness of *style*. People sometimes associate expository preaching with a monotonous sameness of style. It ought to be just the reverse. For the Bible has within it a wide variety of styles. Paul's letter to the Romans is in one style, 1 John in another, Matthew in another, Proverbs in another, Job in another.

Our preaching ought to take not just its content but also its tone and style from the passage. We ought not to preach Job in the same manner as we preach Romans. And if as ministers we are taking the tone and style from our different Bible books, then there will be in the style, manner and tone of our sermons a refreshing variety. I realise that many of us struggle with this, and our sermons do tend to revert to a default style; but consecutive expository ministry can help to free us from this.

6. CONSECUTIVE EXPOSITORY PREACHING MODELS GOOD NOURISHING BIBLE READING FOR THE ORDINARY CHRISTIAN

A topical sermon models for the ordinary Christian a reading of the Bible that consists of dipping in and picking out plums. It seems to be a form of lucky (or unlucky) dip. And even if the topical preaching comes from a minister with a comprehensive lifelong knowledge of scripture, and perfectly maintains the balance of scripture, still the model presented to the ordinary Christian is the lucky dip model.

The knowledge of the Bible that the young Christian acquires from a diet of topical preaching is like the knowledge of London that I acquired as a teenager. When I was old enough to travel on my own on the underground, I used to emerge overground from different stations and get to know little bits of London. I might emerge from Oxford Circus one day and get to know a little of Oxford Street and Regent Street. Then another day I might emerge at Westminster and see where the Houses of Parliament are. But I remember it being an eye-opener to me to discover that these little pockets of familiarity actually joined up overground! I had no sense of how London fitted together. In the same way I may get to know a text like Philippians 4:13, and maybe my eyes might wander briefly to some of the verses nearby. But I have no grasp of how Philippians fits together, let alone of how Philippians might fit into the rest of the Bible's story.

But consecutive exposition says to the ordinary Christian: you too can take Philippians and read quietly through it day by day. You can take Philippians as a project for your personal times of Bible reading and prayer. Live in Philippians for a while. Read it all, and then read it bit by bit, connecting it up. This is a model for Bible reading that will nourish and sustain. Good topical preaching may give a Christian a fish, but good expository ministry will teach him how to fish.

7. CONSECUTIVE EXPOSITORY PREACHING HELPS US PREACH
    THE WHOLE CHRIST FROM THE WHOLE OF SCRIPTURE

I have been thinking that one of the devil's tricks is to reduce 'Jesus' to a mantra. It is worth asking of some songs what difference it would make to change them, if every time the word 'Jesus' appeared we substituted some other word, perhaps 'Buddha' or some random word like 'Dardar'.[6] For some, it might not make much difference, since the word 'Jesus' functions as a meaningless mantra, repeated as though it has some power of its own from the pronunciation of the two syllables.

Part of what brings depth to Christian discipleship is a growing awareness of who Jesus Christ is and what he means, so that the word 'Jesus' really does connect to the person Jesus. The only access we have to the authentic Jesus is from the whole Bible, which is the Father's testimony given by the Spirit to the Son. It follows that we may expect to grow in our knowledge of Jesus as we are taught the whole Bible. Christians who are only ever exposed to part of the Bible are only ever exposed to

---

6.   This word really is meaningless: I made it up.

a truncated Jesus. Our job as preachers is so to proclaim Christ that we may present people mature in him (Col. 1:28-29).

We must therefore seek over time to proclaim as much of Christ as we can to the people we serve, and we will best do this by a diet of carefully planned consecutive expository preaching, in which we seek to cover different kinds of Bible books with the long-term aim of exposing them to as much as we possibly can of the Father's testimony to his beloved Son.

CONCLUSION

I hope these seven blessings of consecutive expository ministry will encourage us to 'give God the microphone'. Let us trust his agenda, not listening to 'relevance', 'entertainment' or 'immediacy'. Let us allow the disciplines of exposition to guard us against reading out of context. Let us be glad that our selectivity is diluted by the disciplines of consecutive exposition. May we and our hearers enjoy a week-by-week freshness of content and style. Let us model for them the kind of nourishing Bible reading by which they themselves can grow. And so let us set before them all of Christ in all of scripture, that we may present them mature in Christ at the end.

PT Media

www.proctrust.org.uk

resources for preachers and Bible Teachers

PT Media, a ministry of *The Proclamation Trust*, provides a range of multimedia resources for preachers and Bible teachers.

Books

The *Teach the Bible* series, published jointly with *Christian Focus Publications*, is specifically geared to the purpose of God's Word – its proclamation as living truth. Written by preachers for preachers, it goes beyond most commentaries to help the reader not only understand the text but to communicate and apply it to real life. Features include:

- Analysis of the overall purpose of the book or biblical theme.
- Advice on planning a preaching series.
- A suggested series, covering the whole book, worked through sermon by sermon.
- Communicating, applying, and illustrating the message.
- Example sermon outlines
- Bible studies

Recent titles are: *Teaching Romans, Teaching Matthew, Teaching John, Teaching Acts, Teaching 1 Peter, Teaching Amos, Teaching Romans,* and *Teaching the Christian Hope.* Forthcoming titles include: *Teaching Mark, Teaching Daniel, Teaching Isaiah, Teaching Nehemiah, Teaching 1, 2, 3 John, Teaching Ephesians, Teaching 1&2 Samuel.*

DVD Training for preachers

Preaching & Teaching the Old Testament:
  Narrative, Prophecy, Poetry, Wisdom

Preaching & Teaching the New Testament:
  Gospels, Epistles, Acts & Revelation

These training DVDs aim to give preachers and teachers confidence in handling the rich variety of God's word. David Jackman has taught this material to generations of students, and he gives us step-by-step instructions on handling each genre of biblical literature.

He demonstrates principles that will guide us through the challenges of teaching and applying different parts of the Bible, for example:

- How does prophecy relate to the lives of its hearers – ancient and modern?
- How can you preach in a way that reflects the deep emotion of the Psalms?

The *Old Testament* set contains four DVDs covering Narrative, Prophecy, Poetry and Wisdom.
The *New Testament* set contains three DVDs, covering Gospels, Letters, Acts and Revelation.

Both sets are suitable for preachers and for those teaching the Bible in a wide variety of contexts.

- Designed for *individual* and *group* study.
- Interactive learning through many *worked examples* and *exercises*
- Flexible format ideal for *training courses*
- Optional *English subtitles* for second-language users.
- Print as many *workbooks* as you need (PDF).

PT Media: Resources for preachers and Bible teachers

Free Audio
PT Media Audio Resources offer a wide range of mp3 downloads for the preacher or Bible teacher, covering over twenty years of conferences.

- *Sermons On…* series (expository sermons).
- **Instruction On…** series (how to teach a Bible book or doctrinal theme).

For further information on these and other PT Media products, visit our website at **www.proctrust.org.uk** or email **media@ proctrust.org.uk**.

ISBN 978-1-84550-255-3

ISBN 978-1-84550-142-6

ISBN 978-1-84550-347-5

ISBN 978-1-85792-790-0

ISBN 978-1-84550-455-7

ISBN 978-1-84550-456-4

Other books from PT Media:

Teaching Acts:
Unlocking the book of Acts for the Bible Teacher
David Cook
ISBN 978-1-84550-255-3

Teaching Amos:
Unlocking the prophecy of Amos for the Bible Teacher
Bob Fyall
ISBN 978-1-84550-142-6

Teaching 1 Peter:
Unlocking the book of I Peter for the Bible Teacher
Angus MacLeay
ISBN 978-1-84550-347-5

Teaching John:
Unlocking the Gospel of John for the Bible Teacher
Dick Lucas & William Philip
ISBN 978-1-85792-790-0

Teaching Matthew:
Unlocking the Gospel of Matthew for the Expositor
David Jackman
ISBN 978-1-85792-877-8

Teaching the Christian Hope:
Unlocking Biblical Eschatology for the Expositor
David Jackman
ISBN 978-1-85792-518-0

Bible Delight:
Psalm 119 for the Bible Teacher and Bible Hearer
Christopher Ash
ISBN 978-1-84550-360-4

Teaching Romans:
Volume 1: Unlocking Romans 1–8 for the Bible Teacher
Christopher Ash
ISBN 978-1-84550-455-7

Teaching Romans:
Volume 2: Unlocking Romans 9–16 for the Bible Teacher
Christopher Ash
ISBN 978-1-84550-464-9

Christian Focus Publications

publishes books for all ages

Our mission statement –

STAYING FAITHFUL
In dependence upon God we seek to impact the world through literature faithful to His infallible Word, the Bible. Our aim is to ensure that the LORD Jesus Christ is presented as the only hope to obtain forgiveness of sin, live a useful life and look forward to heaven with Him.

REACHING OUT
Christ's last command requires us to reach out to our world with His gospel. We seek to help fulfil that by publishing books that point people towards Jesus and help them develop a Christ-like maturity. We aim to equip all levels of readers for life, work, ministry and mission.

Books in our adult range are published in three imprints:

Christian Focus contains popular works including biographies, commentaries, basic doctrine and Christian living. Our children's books are also published in this imprint.

Mentor focuses on books written at a level suitable for Bible College and seminary students, pastors, and other serious readers. The imprint includes commentaries, doctrinal studies, examination of current issues and church history.

Christian Heritage contains classic writings from the past.

Christian Focus Publications Ltd
Geanies House, Fearn,
Ross-shire, IV20 1TW, Scotland, United Kingdom
info@christianfocus.com

Our titles are available from quality bookstores and
www.christianfocus.com